M W
& R

The Good Wine

THE GOOD WINE

An Artist Comes of Age

Doris McCarthy

MACFARLANE WALTER & ROSS
TORONTO

Macfarlane Walter & Ross
37A Hazelton Avenue
Toronto, Canada M5R 2E3

CANADIAN CATALOGUING IN PUBLICATION DATA

McCarthy, Doris, 1910 –
    The good wine.
    Sequel to: A fool in paradise.
    Includes index.

Cloth ISBN 0-921912-21-8
Paperback ISBN 0-921912-36-6

1. McCarthy, Doris, 1910-   . 2. Women painters -
Canada - Biography.   3. Landscape painters -
Canada - Biography.   I. Title.

ND249.M23A2 1991   759.11   C91-094599-3

Printed and bound in Canada

To Marjorie,
and to Virginia and Nancy and Florence,
who lived many of these years with me.

Contents

Illustrations follow pages 136 and 236

Foreword

IT IS A SATISFACTION to be able to bring my story up to date with part two of my autobiography. In this report of the second forty years of my life I have been encouraged and supported by those readers of *A Fool in Paradise* who wrote asking for more. And I have been once more blessed by the perceptive and critical help of that jewel among editors, Jan Walter, who has also maintained for this edition the high standard of design that made part one a visual pleasure. My thanks are offered to the artists and groups of artists, the book clubs and writers' groups who received the Fool so graciously and welcomed a new author into their company. It is my hope that you will enjoy reading about these four decades as much as I enjoyed living them and telling you about them.

1

The Good Wine

TURNING FORTY SHOULD have been traumatic. I remember finding the very word forty difficult as a child. Why did it have no *u* in it when both four and fourteen met rational expectations? As I grew older, although the spelling still gives me pause, forty took on a new aura. It was middle age. One adage has it that life begins at forty, but observation told me that it is the time when women search the mirror for the first grey hair and men start to bulge at belt level. True, it can be a beginning, a moment of truth when youth is gently relinquished, when goals are re-evaluated and changes made while there is still time.

So it was for me. The year that would see me pass that landmark, 1950, promised great things. Since 1932, when I first began teaching, I had been struggling up a long dark tunnel crowded with obstacles that took all my strength and ingenuity to get by. There was beautiful light at the far end, but I knew that the tunnel was forty (that number again) years long and I had not yet reached the half-way point. Suddenly the tunnel turned a corner and there was an opening. Ahead of me I could see release: a sabbatical leave, a full year when I would be free of teaching, free to stop hurrying, free to paint, to breathe deeply, and to look about. It would be an opportunity to step back from my life, question the path I had chosen, speculate about alternatives, find out what it felt like to be a full-time artist, try emotional freedom and compare it with my commitment to the man who had filled my horizon for most of the previous ten years. This leave, shared with a friend who was a colleague and fellow artist, was to be an adventure of travel and study that we were to call in retrospect our "wonderful year."

It really began on the winter day when I went after school to Ginny's house to plan the details. Ginny was Virginia Luz, also a teacher in the art department of Central Technical School in Toronto. I had been appointed to the staff in the early thirties, soon after graduating from the Ontario College of Art. Seven years later Ginny was taken into the department to replace Noreen Masters, who lost her job as a matter of routine when she married. Through the long strained years of the war, when several of the men on our staff were off being war artists, Ginny and I had become friends. We had shared many painting trips to Haliburton and the Gaspé coast before we cooked up this wonderful idea of a year abroad together.

Ginny was a former graduate of the department, a slim dark girl, smart in high heels, wearing her clothes with flair, a pleasure to look at. She had grown up during the

Depression, when her father was out of work and the cupboard at home sometimes literally bare. She once said that when she began to earn a salary, all the money she had left after helping at home went on her back. One of the subjects she taught was fashion drawing, and she looked the part.

We had been granted leave together and were told late in December 1949 that our year off was to start the following June, twelve months earlier than we had expected. The veterans' rehabilitation classes, which had been organized after the war to give the young men and women in the services the educational opportunities they had missed by enlisting, were to be terminated at that time. The war artists were back, and until Edna Jutton's retirement the following year the department would be overstaffed. We could be spared in 1950 better than later. We were thrown into a happy frenzy by this sudden change of timetable.

I had been teaching for all those years without a break, slugging my slow way from a timetable loaded with vocational students who had neither talent nor interest in art to a program that included painting classes for the senior art students. The work had become richer and more satisfying but also heavier and more demanding. And I was determined to earn from the students the same respect they had felt for the men I was replacing, Charles Goldhamer, Carl Schaefer, and Cavin Atkins, who were well-known exhibiting artists. To establish my own status I had, since 1930, entered every juried exhibition within reach and organized my own solo shows in Toronto and wherever else I saw an opportunity. In 1944 I had achieved membership in the Ontario Society of Artists, all the while carrying a heavy teaching load and managing a tumultuous personal life.

The sudden prospect of freedom raised us to the heights, but a leisurely year and a half of planning and preparing was reduced to a few months. Could we find the money? was the first question. Virginia had few savings, and the half-salary she would be drawing while on leave would not go far enough, but her brother Edgar rose to the occasion with a generous loan that made up the difference. I cashed in my war savings, and we both began pinching pennies.

Leaving the responsibilities of our homes and families was the next challenge. The housekeeper Ginny had engaged when her mother first took ill had remained after Mrs. Luz died, and would look after Edgar and their eighty-one-year-old father. My mother was still able to manage her own home, but a fall down my cellar stairs a year earlier had resulted in a serious back injury that had taken its toll. I knew that she was far more dependent on me than she had been before. However, my lifelong friend Marjorie, who was more like a sister to me than a friend, had known her almost as long and almost as well as I did. She and her husband, Roy Wood, lived just two streets away from Mother and would keep a eye on her.

Hardest of all to leave was my home, Fool's Paradise. The original cottage, stark in an empty field beside a poplar copse, with the deep Bellamy Ravine on one side and a sheer drop to Lake Ontario in front, was gradually becoming my dream house. It had been enlarged by the addition of a studio and garage, softened with flower-beds and shrubbery, set out with fruit trees, and bordered with pines and maples that were already promising to become tall trees. I was permanently in love with the place, but I tried to hold it lightly, and I had learned long since that when you choose what you want most in life, you must not begrudge the price. My one-time camp friends Margaret Cork and Gwen Oliver agreed to live in my house and adopt my cats. I knew they would love it and them.

Our intention was to drive about in our own automobile in Britain and Europe, painting as we went. We made a date with a car salesman, who was to meet us at Ginny's place one winter afternoon and explain how we could buy an Austin in Canada and have it delivered to the boat on our arrival in Liverpool. For Ginny this would be a first car, an exciting thought, and both of us were keyed up with the tension of such a major purchase. After we signed for a four-door hatchback and parted with a substantial cheque, about nine hundred dollars each, more than two months' salary then, I stayed on at Virginia's for dinner. Afterwards we spread out the maps on the dining-room table and thrashed out a general plan for the year. We decided on Britain for the summer and fall, northern Europe until Christmas, then south to Italy and France. The very names were magic. In 1935, when I had been studying in England, there had been neither time nor money for such adventure, and to Ginny it was all unknown territory. Our excitement mounted as the plan took shape. When I had gathered up the papers and driven off in my jeep, Ginny's brother Edgar said to her, "Are you really going to spend a year with *her*?"

"Why not?" asked Ginny in surprise.

"You fought all the time," said Ed.

"That wasn't fighting," said Ginny. "We were just discussing."

There were many more hot discussions, but never any fighting. I am quick to seize on an idea or a plan and ready to adopt it immediately. Ginny says no at once, to slow me up and give herself time to think it over. I let her warm up to the idea until we can talk it through and come to some agreement. We had no problems that could not be resolved by compromise; we both valued peace more than getting our own way.

One of my nagging worries about going to England so soon after the war, while rationing was still in force, was that cigarettes would be scarce and I would waste precious time chasing them. I was not a heavy smoker, never so much as a pack a day, but I was addicted, quite equal to getting dressed in the middle of the night to drive up to Kingston Road if I found myself out of the weed. This was in the back of my mind that New Year's day of 1950 as I sat in front of my fire at Fool's Paradise leafing through a *Reader's Digest* that somebody had left at Christmas. In it was an interim report published by a team of doctors who were doing a six-year research project on the effects of smoking on health. Only two years of their six were complete, but they had already made such alarming discoveries that they felt they could not wait six years to let people know. I read it through, stubbed out the cigarette I was smoking, and promised myself not to have another until my birthday the following July. Birthdays and Christmas I would allow myself one cigarette, and with that carrot dangling in front of me I took my courage in hand to conquer the habit. It was not easy. For a few days not smoking was a full-time job, which I survived by following the cats around the house with a sketch-book and a stick of conté crayon, something to do with my hands. Ginny stopped smoking at the same time, but weakened, and I used to find the smell of her cigarettes a consolation. Even second-hand smoke was better than nothing.

The spring was full of goodbye parties, ending with a gala farewell organized by the art department, featuring student skits based on our probable adventures abroad. I seem to remember camels and pyramids as well as a full-sized two-dimensional jeep, which lived in my garage with its prototype for many years afterwards. A few days before the end of term Peter Haworth, head of the art department, who had been so co-operative about letting us both go at the same time, put Ginny and me side by side against the wall of the stairwell leading up to the life-drawing room and solemnly traced an outline around each of us. "Just make sure that you fit into that when you come back," he said.

Our send-off gathering at Toronto's Union Station included Ginny's father with her housekeeper and a cluster of friends, my mother, supported morally and physically by Marjorie and Roy, and some of my faithful "Shawnees," once my Bible class and CGIT group. It was an emotional parting even though everyone was trying to be cheerful and brave. A year is a long time when parents are elderly. As the train jerked into motion and pulled slowly away, everyone waved and continued waving until we were out of sight. Then Ginny and I looked at each other and began to grin. I think those grins were permanent for the whole fourteen months.

We were a day ahead of our sailing deadline, unwilling to take any chance of missing the boat at Montreal and

horrified by the news that a sister ship, the *Franconia*, had
run aground on the Isle d'Orleans the day we left home.
But no mishap marred our voyage or made it memorable,
except the pathetic, middle-aged, hard-drinking mother's
boy from Portland, Oregon, who was our table companion for any meal that he did not sit out in the bar.

Expecting to be met by our own car, we had organized
our clothing and equipment for the year into small units,
easy to handle, easy to categorize and to pack into the
trunk and back seat. But we were met instead by the news
that some necessary papers had not been provided by us
and there would be no car until we had completed these
documents and had them notarized. Notarized? In Liverpool, a strange city, on a Friday afternoon? What a
hope! We gathered together our seventeen small pieces
of luggage, including a fruit basket that someone had sent
to the boat, still with its one last banana, and found a
porter to take the collection to Left Luggage while we
retired with our maps to a café for a conference. How
could we get out of this big industrial city and salvage the
weekend? We discovered that Chester, a medieval walled
town, was almost on the doorstep, just eighteen miles
south. What life was taking with one hand, it was offering
back with the other.

An hour later the same porter was reassembling the
seventeen pieces. "Where you goin', Miss?"

"Chester."

"And how long you stayin'?"

"Till Monday." His eyes popped, but he was game.

"I'll hump while you counts."

The seventeen pieces, minus the banana mysteriously
vanished, were put on a train with us and eventually

carried out of the Chester station and across the road to the Queen's Hotel by a procession of porters and bootboys. By this time we were beyond feeling ludicrous.

Our notary, when we located one on Monday, was straight out of Dickens. He peered at us through square, steel-rimmed spectacles across a shabby desk surrounded by shelves of books so aged that their leather backs were rotting away. As he read aloud to us, slowly and carefully, every word of both copies of the forms we had brought him, we gave up any hope of quick action in getting our car and decided to cross over to Ireland without it. The Queen's Hotel gave us a "drummer's" room in which to spread out our belongings for a complete re-sorting, and agreed to store the surplus until our return. We were informed that drummers were not musicians but English salesmen who travelled around "drumming up" business.

After a swing south from Dublin in a rented automobile, we settled into a small hotel in Connemara in country full of thatched crofts and peat bogs ringed by low mountains. We began painting. For a frustrating few days I tried to work with casein, new to me but highly recommended. It is an opaque water-colour, latex based, but the latex clogged my brushes, demanding a thorough washing with soap or detergent every few minutes to keep them pliable. I gave up and changed back to familiar water-colour. The other hazard of painting in Connemara was the weather. Every ten minutes the light changed, the sun hiding behind clouds that then spilled on us. We would scramble to the car to protect our wet paintings, and would just have opened our whodunnits when the sun would return, flooding the world with such a glory of colour that we raced out and set up easels and chairs once

more. Folding aluminum chairs were unknown in Britain
in 1950, and ours occasioned great interest and some
covetousness wherever we went.

It was while we were painting in Connemara that we
met Goyo Bouvy, a Dutch visitor of about our own age
who had lived through the German occupation as an
underground worker. She was tall, with fair hair and skin,
very Nordic, reserved, sitting by herself at table and
content to spend the days alone, hiking or exploring the
country by bus. But she accepted our overtures, and at
her invitation we added Hoorn, the medieval town where
she lived in Holland, to our European plans.

Those days painting in Ireland would have been idyl-
lically happy if I could have relaxed and been content to
record the country and the weather. Instead, I kept demanding of myself that I should be producing Great Art,
and failing as usual to appreciate the good qualities of
what I was doing. Later I could see that my sketches did
capture the moodiness of the constantly changing light
and the unaccustomed brilliance of the wet Irish colour.

When we returned to England after a fortnight and
found ourselves still without a car, our patience gave out
and we made up our minds to go to London to the Austin
head office and demand action. London had not been on
our schedule until late autumn. But we discovered that
by train from Chester we could be there in four hours.
London – after all those years!

The city had been home to me for a year back in 1935
when I had lived there with Noreen Masters and George
Keith-Beattie. We had been in England for post-graduate
study at the Central School of Arts and Crafts a couple
of years before Nory and George were married. One of

the friends we made then and had kept ever since was Robert Watson, "Scotty" to us. When I phoned to say that Virginia and I were on our way, he and his wife Anne invited us to spend the weekend at their home in East Croydon and to take a Saturday tour of London under his guidance. Once more we boarded the train at Chester, but this time with one small suitcase each and London our goal. We came out of Victoria Station just as Big Ben began to strike. To Ginny, this was the voice that had reached her in Canada all through the time that her brother Edgar was in the army overseas. It held the memories and emotion of those terrible years. She stood motionless and speechless, tears running down her face.

After a proper tourist's Saturday with the sights of London, Scotty and Anne gave us an English Sunday, with cricket on the green and afternoon tea at the local club. On Monday it was down to business.

My diary, trusty companion, recorder, and commentator, reported briefly. "August 14, 1950: To Oxford Street with blood in our eyes – Mr. Rogers, manager, just too gracious, blood subsided – delivery promised for that very afternoon."

Once in our own car, Chester having been revisited to recover the luggage, we explored and painted, painted and explored, as far west as Land's End and up into Scotland, doing a routine of ancestor-hunting in Mac-Donald country for Ginny as we had done in County Cork in Ireland for me. We fell in love with East Anglia and heard our first nightingale in a back lane near Long Melford. We untangled some of the difficulties inevitable in such intimate and interdependent living. From time to time, if we felt the tensions mounting, either between us

or in frustration over our work, we would declare Sunday
and take a day of rest. Our favourite way of spending it
was in cleaning out the car and reorganizing all our
belongings. Both Ginny and I love order, and we were
quickly exhausted by confusion. Early on we had agreed
that each of us should feel free to go to church (me) or
stay home (Ginny) with no sense of guilt for having
abandoned the other. And we laughed at the same things.

One of our mutual pleasures was eavesdropping.
When we ate in hotels or restaurants, we ate in silence,
fascinated by the conversations at the tables within ear-
shot.

"September 3: Listened in on impassioned family ar-
gument about whether or no Martin, who seemed to be
about eleven, had a classical or mechanical brain and
could ever become an admiral of the fleet."

A day of great celebration was the Tuesday after the
Canadian Labour Day, end of the holidays at home, when
we were not starting another school year. We emphasized
our freedom by following friends at Central Tech all day
in our thoughts as we drove over the Yorkshire moors,
ending up at Ilkley Moor as a special tribute to Dawson
Kennedy, best-loved of our colleagues back home and
noted for his rendition of the song *Ilkley Moor bar t'at*.

Coming south to Stratford-on-Avon, we saw the current play, *Henry VIII*, in the Memorial Theatre. It was the
first time that the Stratford theatre had abandoned the
proscenium stage, and the production even for England
was revolutionary. There was no curtain. The set was
open to view when we came into the auditorium, banners
in place and stirring in a breeze from the wings, already
alive. Canada had known nothing like this. We were

enthralled, and agreed that it was the best Shakespeare
we had ever seen.

Cornwall and Devon offered fishing villages, familiar
from our days on the Gaspé but new because of the
distinctive architecture. Ginny's painstaking attention to
every pane of glass in every window of every house on
the headland at Mevagissey gave us a new word for our
common language. If one of us even today is bogging
down in fussy details, the other need say only
"Mevagissey" and the message is clear.

My diary is full of the cathedrals and churches and the
early services I attended. We had been impressed by
Chester Cathedral on our first weekend in England, and
not just because we were still feeling the motion of the
boat and could see the Gothic arches swaying above us.
Ginny said that her knees buckled when she looked up.
Afterwards, when we met that experience of being over-
whelmed by grandeur and beauty, we said "It did a
cathedral to me."

I had been teaching history of art, including the Gothic,
and studying many of these buildings from mean little
engravings in textbooks. It made a great difference to
meet the real thing, and it made even more of a difference
to experience it in action, to feel the building vibrate to
the organ, to share the silences, to delight in the cadence
of a scholarly sermon and the unique sound of the boy
choristers, on one occasion even to smell the real thing.

We were in York for a big county-wide service in the
Minster, attended by all the mayors and bigwigs of the
area and patronized by royalty. They arrived directly
from a banquet at the Guild-hall and moved down the
centre aisle, a stately procession in full regalia, colourful

academic robes, medieval dress for the lord mayor, chains of office and staffs, all heralded by a great crescendo of music from the organ and accompanied, as it drew near to us, by a rich aroma of scotch whisky. It must have been quite a banquet.

Back in London early in October we found and settled into the Portland Court Hotel, two town houses that once had belonged to the Duke of Portland, now joined to become a small hotel on Queen's Gate just south of Hyde Park and Kensington Gardens. It was respectable, a bit shabby after the war but inexpensive, and soon felt like home to us. Many of the guests were permanent residents, most of whom seemed to be gentry in reduced circumstances, some of them recently home from India, displaced by the British withdrawal. It was like living in the play *Separate Tables*. The dining-room was crowded, with the tables separate, yes, but so close to each other that only British reserve and respect for privacy kept the conversations apart. Sheilagh, the red-haired Irish waitress, reacting to our friendly interest and praise of Ireland, made sure that we had enough butter (still rationed) and generally treated us as favoured guests. Most of the residents showed her a contempt that she fully returned.

At four o'clock a tea-wagon was wheeled into the lounge, and some resident poured for whoever was there. It was black comedy to watch the manoeuvring to secure a chair close to the tea-wagon so that your tea was first brew and not the wet-and-weak that followed as more and more hot water was added to the pot. Ginny and I laughed at the ploys, but we also suspected that some of the poor old souls couldn't afford our option of going out and paying for good tea elsewhere.

This was a different London from the one I had known when I was there as a student fifteen years earlier. Dear Major Balbernie, who had been all important to me that year, was gone, a victim of the Norwegian campaign in 1941. His sister Kitty took us to her heart for his sake, and we loved her for her own. She was a witchlike little woman, bent, shabby, with unkempt grey hair, peering at the world through thick glasses from her cushion on the floor among her books. She subsisted in a miserable little bed-sitter, making tea on a hotplate on the floor, insisting that Ginny and I should sit on her one chair and the bed, talking without pause of her delight in seeing us, full of admiration for everything about us and our work, and buoyant with hope of the great things that were going to happen to her as a result of the writing she was currently doing for the British Broadcasting Corporation. She lived on crumbs literally and metaphorically.

This time London meant theatre. We saw T.S. Eliot's *Cocktail Party* on its first run, and *Ring around the Moon* with Claire Bloom. Prices were low by Canadian standards, and we bought tickets for a second performance before we left the theatre.

My biggest excitement was a luncheon date with Dorothy L. Sayers. Marjorie and I had read all her detective stories, falling in love with Lord Peter Wimsey and the England he lived in. We had then gone on to read her more recent books, the translations of Dante, and her religious plays. *The Mind of the Maker*, which explored the trinitarian nature of creativity, was already one of my permanent treasures. A group of like-minded at St. Aidan's Church at home had gathered every Sunday evening one spring to listen together to the broadcasts of

her radio play *Man Born To Be King*. When things were at
their worst during the war I had written to her, and her
acknowledgement came on a lino print, her own work.
This was my field. I realized that since her lino block was
nothing extraordinary, perhaps she was only human, with
needs like any ordinary person, and sent her some parcels
of hard-to-come-by foods that were still available in Canada. Her letters of thanks gave me courage to ask to meet
her, and this invitation to join her for lunch in London
was the result.

She was a hard-working writer, sparing a precious hour
from the play she was completing for Colchester's two-
thousand-year anniversary celebration. She was also a
shy, very private person, probably appalled at the prospect
of having to entertain this strange female from the colo-
nies. She brought with her Muriel St. Clare Byrne, another writer and a woman of so much warmth and charm
that there was no possibility of awkwardness in her company. Muriel was a specialist in Shakespeare, and pleased
by my enthusiasm about the open staging of *Henry VIII* that
Ginny and I had seen at Stratford. The talk was wide-
ranging and lively, and we all had a good time.

The following summer Ginny and I were able to be at
the opening night of the Colchester play, to hear Sayers
speak afterwards, and to join the many others who were
anxious to congratulate her. It's the only lion-hunting I
have ever done. I still marvel that I had the temerity, and
rejoice that I did it.

When our scheduled time in England was up, the prospect of leaving its dear familiarity for the continent was

traumatic, especially for Virginia, who is by nature less adventurous than I. But we were invited to spend a night or two with the Dutch family who had become Edgar's friends when he was part of the Canadian army of liberation. Twello, where they lived, was a tiny village, and to make it easy to find their house, Di Ankersmidt had planted a large red ensign (Canada's flag at that time) on the lawn. Their welcome was heart-warming. And they were such hospitable, loving people that we stayed with them for almost a month, painting in the countryside nearby and visiting the museums and art galleries within range. Di collected clocks, and every hour there would be a two- or three-minute concert as they struck or chimed not quite in sync. Jekke, his beautiful wife, was as fluent in French and English as in Dutch, and completely charming in each. They told us harrowing stories of the war, still vividly present to them. One of their younger sons was having a hard time adjusting to the sudden shift in moral codes that peace had brought. During the occupation he had been encouraged to lie and steal from the Germans, and now he was confused by the whole changed set of ethics.

After two weeks' painting around Twello we drove up to Hoorn to visit Goyo, approaching it by a long dike across the Zuider Zee and nibbling on liqueur chocolates, Jekke's parting gift. Driving into this ancient town, we found all the old buildings leaning out into the street, and for a few minutes we were not sure whether the architecture or the chocolates might be responsible for the strangeness.

Goyo lived on the top floor of an ancient half-tower on the quay. Its rounded side was to sea, its flat face turned

towards the town and leaning forward. From its windows
we watched the drama on Saint Nicholas day.

"The streets were thronged with children. Up in the
tower we hung out the windows and saw them scram-
bling and slipping on the wet boards of the derelict
wooden quay, and even smaller children by the score and
hundreds on the sea-wall – sometimes accompanied by
adults, sometimes precariously on their own. Finally the
ship came with a flutter of pennants from bow to mast
and mast to stern, with a brave wake behind it. St. Nick,
in a white robe with a red cloak and mitre and a silky
white beard, was waving to the children, attended by
Black Piet in lilac doublet and short jacket, and four little
(and very black) pages. The excitement among the children grew as the ship neared the narrows, and reached a
noisy peak as it passed in. There was a band to greet it,
leading a company of red-coated and red-cocked-hatted
soldiers, followed by a coach with white horses and
footmen ready for the saint, as well as a black shiny car
for the burgomaster and mere civic officials."

The next day we went walking in fog so thick that a
half-seen movement down the street frightened us. There
was a strange knot of people forming and separating,
struggling together, almost merging, breaking apart and
rushing at each other again. Our heads were still full of
war stories. As we drew near it was a relief to discover
that it was a wedding group posing for photographs.

To leave Holland, Goyo, the Ankersmidts, and all the
Dutch friends of theirs who had treated us as if we two
personally had been their liberators, was hard. But to
venture into Germany, land of the enemy in two world
wars, was even harder, and I marvel that we went at all.

Jekke couldn't bring herself to talk about our going there. She had been fluent in German but said she would never speak it again. No wonder Ginny had a bilious attack to mark our crossing.

The border formalities under the eyes of armed guards were nerve-racking. It was snowing, which added to the sense of threat. But almost as soon as we were in Germany we felt a difference. It was shabbier but more beautiful, and everywhere there were Christmas trees, complete with candles and angels.

The next day the snow had stopped, and I determined to get on with something I had promised to do for a friend back home. Her son had been shot down in a plane over a little village called Pattern. He was presumed dead, but she was haunted by the fear that he was perhaps wounded and with memory loss, or carried off to Russia. Would I try to find out what had really happened to the crew of that aircraft?

We found Pattern. Ginny, sick, miserable, and frightened, burrowed into her rug and declined to get out of the car. I walked until I saw someone to speak to. "Burgomaster?" He shook his head. Thank God for gestures. I pointed ahead, behind, to the right and left, repeating, "Burgomaster?" He understood me, and came with me to show me the way. He guided me through a bolted wooden door that led to a courtyard and around to the back of the house. A small white dog leapt against his chain and barked and barked. It was a big, awkward, very German-looking burgomaster who admitted me and showed me into a tiny office. His unhealthy-looking son came too, and I tried to explain my visit, but neither could understand what I was asking, and we seemed to be at an impasse. I used mime, and they confirmed that a plane had crashed in Pattern. Their gestures made me think they knew where, perhaps had seen it, but my problem was far too subtle for our mutual vocabulary.

The burgomaster went to look for a man who could speak French. His son turned the office upside-down in search of an English-German dictionary. Eventually the burgomaster returned with his nephew, a handsome, well-built lad, probably about thirty, with a dictionary under his arm and a rueful disclaimer about his English. However, he knew just enough. I wrote out sentences. We looked up any doubtful word, and they assured me that they had seen the plane crash, and that all were killed. Then the three of us walked up the hill outside the village to where the plane had fallen. The path led through a vegetable-garden plot. When the nephew found the gate locked, he lifted it quickly and confidently out of its hinges, explaining with a laugh, "I am a soldier."

We stood in the snowy field with bare trees along the fence line, and they showed me how it had come, where it had struck, where the engine had buried itself two metres down, here one wing and here the other, and the explosion that blew the poor crew apart and consumed them in fire. The German had been a pilot over Russia. He asked me "How old?" "Twenty-three." He shook his head. "It is war," and added, "The people don't want war. It is the officers. They say go and we go," and he hunched up and jog-trotted a bit in parody of how the little people obey. We shook hands all round and I climbed in with Ginny, beside myself with the strangeness of the experience, the shabby, damaged village, pathetic and rather beautiful, the two kindly men, one so clumsy and helpless but willing, the other so charming and helpful and willing too. Being in Germany at all was an emotional upheaval.

"Dusseldorf, December 9, 1950: This moment I am so happy that I just have to write. Ginny and I went to evensong this afternoon, found our way through Carlyle House [a kind of club for the British, who were responsible for this area of Germany, still under supervision after the war], down a dark spiral staircase and into an austere but rather pleasant chapel, where we joined two yawning females and a sweet, somewhat deaf priest in saying evensong and came out feeling a sudden release of tensions and a flood of homecoming. Ginny said the same thing over our beer at supper later on. It's worth missing church, as I have been, to have her discover that she misses it too. Dusseldorf is no longer a desolate, broken, sad, sinister city – it's almost Jerusalem."

We had chosen to reach Oberammergau late in December because we judged that it should be able to offer us a real Christmas. And indeed it did. We stayed at a pension with the widow of the man who had played Christ in the passion play for many years. Her daughter and son-in-law and their children lived with her, and also Tante Anne, who became our friend and mentor. An elderly sister of the widow, she had taught in England before the war, and her savings had vanished in the great money devaluation at its end. Her English was beautiful, but it was her German that we appreciated. She spoke German to us always. We answered as best we could. She corrected us. We tried again and again, until we were speaking to her standard. Her nephew was a potter with a kiln out back, and when he heard that we were from Toronto in Canada, he asked us if we knew the gift shop on Yonge Street to which he sold some of his work from time to time. His "gift shop" was Eaton's.

On Christmas Eve we joined the stream of villagers walking through the sparkling cold night to the parish church. We had been warned that all the seats in the nave would be taken and that we must find room on a bench in the gallery. It was a vantage point from which to survey the whole fascinating scene, the high ceiling vibrant with flying angels and cherubs, the densely packed congregation down below us, the two Christmas trees beside the chancel with their real candles burning, alarming in spite of the firemen in red helmets with flaring brims elbowing their way back and forth through the crowded aisles. There was a full orchestra, and the music was traditional, a setting of the mass that had been written by a local musician over a hundred years ago and used every Christmas since that time. Besides the priest there were twelve boy acolytes in red cassocks, with white lace cottas and ski boots. There were twelve red-upholstered stools for them too. And the last time they all filed from the vestry into the chancel, the two who were due to stand at the door with the collection plates were wearing red mittens.

When we came out into the night, the stars were thick and brilliant in the dark sky, and the churchyard was twinkling with candles on all the small Christmas trees that had been set up on the graves, a lovely way of including the friends and family who lay buried there.

From Germany we drove through Austria, painting as we went. There had been rumours of unrest in Germany when we were in the north. The isolated position of Berlin was causing tensions, and we had shared the uneasiness, but we were able to forget it in Bavaria. We remembered it again one afternoon when we had driven out from the village we were staying in and settled down to work beside the road. A car drove up, and three uniformed men jumped out and set up a barricade across the road just behind us, stopping cars and buses as they came along. Mobilization? War again? We were terrified. Our sketches went berserk. I gave up trying to paint and walked along to the men to see if they would tell me what had happened. What had happened was the new year, and they were checking the car licences to see that they were up to date.

A snowstorm held us up in Austria. "Snow – that's the whole news of the day. We walked up the hill this afternoon, and as soon as we were past the church and the farm, we stepped out of life into white, just white, no sky or earth or air or past or present." Our footprints were buried in fresh snow so quickly that we dared not go on.

The next morning the sky was clear, and fence-posts had tops of white snow a metre high. Two days later, when we heard that the roads were open, we bought chains for the tires to give us traction, and started out. But Ginny was nervous at the pace I was maintaining on the snowy roads, and when I slowed down on a curve to spare her, we dug in and couldn't get started again. We were high on a mountain, beyond habitation, beyond help. There were no boughs within reach to pack under the wheels. All we had was our luggage. We unpacked our clothing and spread it on the snow as far as it would stretch, then slowly and carefully, in low low gear, moved the car forward until we were past the curve and on a stretch where we thought we could get started and keep going. Our garments were rescued, shaken, and repacked, little the worse for wear.

Dino Rigolo was waiting for us in northern Italy at his aunt and uncle's farmhouse. Dino was a talented Italian-Canadian art student at Central Tech who had been drafted into the army right from school. After the war he had come back to finish his course in the rehabilitation classes and been kept on as a member of the art staff to replace Dawson Kennedy when Dawson went off on his sabbatical in 1947. Dino was now doing post-graduate study in his native Italy. We were eager to see him again and intended to take him along to be our guide on the way to Rome. Dino was still on his Canada Fellowship, living so carefully that his money was stretching to a second year of study, and this opportunity to see Italy with us was a great treat for him. Having him as a companion was an even greater treat for us. He was merry, enthusiastic, knowledgeable, and young. Dino knew how to find inexpensive hotels for us wherever we went, and even cheaper rooms nearby for him so that he could afford to travel with us and show us the marvels that he knew were waiting in Italy.

The farmhouse interlude proved to be a strain. Dino's uncle was poor, the house tiny. Ginny and I had to share the one big bed with our hostess and her small daughter, while Dino and his uncle were in the other room, probably on the floor. Ginny was again bilious, in a pattern that was beginning to be recognizable as border-crossing nerves. However, as guests, we were on show and had to

remain vertical and smiling no matter how weak and
feeble we felt. We were glad to get on our way and find
the sanctuary of a hotel room with indoor plumbing.
Venice restored us.

"January 8, 1951: Breakfast this morning was as if
someone was pouring health, strength, and comfort into
me. Delicious crusty rolls. Good apricot conserve. Lots
of butter, and the best pot of tea since Twello. G's interior
purred too, and we started off in Venice in fine fettle.
What a day we had, arm in arm, up and over bridges,
pausing for a glance at the green, smooth water, squeez-
ing Dino's arm in sheer enthusiasm at the twist of a
gondola's prow, through streets like alleys, to the Piazza
San Marco, there in the life, sun on the domes, pigeons
on the pavement like flies along the Gaspé sand."

"Ravenna, January 10: A day written in gold mosaics.
We went out for breakfast this morning to a little bar
across the corner, where they had a small boy to send out
for butter, and a black kitten with shiny silk fur and round
yellow eyes (and a low bill). Then we walked down to
San Vitale. We arrived just as the guard came to open the
door, and we went into a round gloom, and turned right,
to the apse, and there it was – glory – magnificence, the
panels of the Emperor Justinian and Empress Theodora
with their attendants, so familiar from reproduction, and
so new. It hit me with the same impact as the nave of Ely
or the interior of Chester or the *Messiah* with Sir Malcolm
Sargent, and I stood with tears running after each other,
hot down my cheeks, and grateful that none of us wanted
to talk about it or even to share the first look. That came
later, when we were a bit more used to it."

I look back on Italy as a wonderful month of walking

with Dino, one of us held firmly on each arm, all laughing. We tramped miles along Roman streets, with sudden stops in front of each fresh masterpiece of architecture or sculpture or to read the posted menu and decide if it came within our budget. We saw the textbook glories and saw some of them adventurously. It was winter. Italy had no central heating in the out-of-the-way places we could afford. In a trattoria in Tarquinia, where we went one weekend to see the Etruscan tombs, we were given small pottery braziers to hold between the knees to fight the chill. In that same ancient town the beds, which had not been slept in since the summer, were as cold and damp as the weather. Even wearing our fur coats, putting extra blankets under us, and rolling our bedding around us wasn't enough. Daylight and getting up were like a release from prison.

Late in January we all went to Florence and were predictably enthralled. And from there we worked our way north and towards the Costa dei Fiori, where, Dino promised us, "the sun always shines." We would be there for the carnival. Dino entertained us with stories of the excitement and gaiety of carnival time in Italy until we were avid.

On our first two days and nights on the Costa it poured with rain. "You see," said Dino, "I *told* you the sun always shines here." But even in the rain we found consolations. My diary betrays as much interest in food as in painting, with fewer poor meals than spoiled sketches. One afternoon, when Dino had put his finished painting down behind the car, I inadvertently backed over it. He laughed as he rescued it and held it up for inspection. "Everything helps," he said. It became our comforting byword.

"Alassio, February 1: Off for a walk all through town to see the carnival excitement – empty streets, utter silence." The laughter was all ours, the joke definitely on us. But I remember the sense of high occasion as the three of us marched down the centre of the dark street, arm in arm, our footsteps on the pavement echoing hollowly, conscious that it was Dino's last night with us and that we would be seeing him off by bus in the morning to return to his studies.

For Ginny and me it was on to France, to St. Tropez, where Monsieur and Madame Sorrieux had been warned of our coming. Mme Sorrieux was the sister of one of my adult students at CTS. Her husband was retired from some high position in the Paris police force. My first impression was of a tall, sweet-faced man with white hair and very blue eyes, and a small, quick, white-haired woman, both struggling with a wild little brown and white cocker spaniel. They were a lovable couple who made us welcome and helped us to find a quayside apartment to rent for a month. The spaniel was the worst-behaved dog we met in all our travels, but he was adored by his owners, and amiable in his naughtiness. He came with them when they brought us baskets of oranges and almonds from their garden, and demanded so boisterously to be taken out that Monsieur spent his visits toiling up and down the four flights of stairs to our eyrie.

Through the windows of our apartment we could watch the tops of the tall masts of the sailboats bobbing in the harbour. The life of the yacht society was spread below for our entertainment. From the balcony we looked down into a wonderful world of sharp white hulls against deep green water and out beyond the yachts to a background of mountains and clouds. We revelled in having our own place after the months of visiting and living in hotels or pensions.

On one of the picnics we shared with her Madame Sorrieux brought a bottle of delicious wine from their own vineyard, assuring us, "It's just pure fruit, you know." I remember her with amusement and affection whenever I offer the same reassurance to my guests today as I ply them with Chateau Fool's Paradise rhubarb wine.

"We spent the morning deliciously, paying our rent, shopping in the rain, with an interval for mid-morning snack, and watching spectacular bursts of sun through the clouds. Then after lunch we sallied forth, up the nearest street and down the alley to where I had done my first painting. Both of us did fair sketches, and both of us had a lovely time. We have done so much delighted housekeeping since moving in that I'm relieved to feel that we haven't forgotten entirely how to paint."

The work I did that month is different from any of my work before or since, higher keyed, full of light and lyrical colour. At the time, as usual, I was in despair because I didn't know how to get down on paper what I saw and felt. Today I am surprised by how much I did manage to say.

"February 13: I ended up on the big shelf of rock in front of Miss McCormick's house, and almost did a winner. It's so maddening when a potentially good sketch is spoiled by one or two bad passages. G was fed up with hers again, so when we were finished, we went marketing together and then out to La Plage for lunch. The new big oranges we bought are the best I've ever tasted. G asked me over lunch what I thought was the meaning of life. I

wondered, even as I answered, if anyone could know who
is sitting in luxurious idleness on a crumbly bit of shore
with the blue, blue Mediterranean slipping and sliding in
over the rocks, full of French bread with much butter and
cheese and jam, and these super-oranges. Surely it's all
too easy this year. The catechism used to say that the chief
end of man is to glorify God and to enjoy Him forever. To
glorify God, how do we do it this year? To enjoy Him
forever? Certainly in Italy I felt as if in the mosaics I was
enjoying Him. The answer is so trite, so true, and so
impertinent."

The days passed in golden contentment, but I had a
secret nag. We had turned west after Italy, away from
Greece, and when would I ever get to Greece if we kept
moving farther and farther from it? Ginny didn't feel
passionate about Greece, but I was steeped in its sculpture and architecture, and longed to see it. In this mood
I was following Ginny over the rocks along the shore one
morning, in search of the day's sketch, when I noticed –
litter? –a paper out of place. It proved to be a travel folder
about Athens. I felt my stomach or heart or something
contract. While we both painted, I brooded, and when
we sat together with our sandwiches at lunch-time, I
broached the subject. How would she feel about flying
back to Athens for a few days?

"Not me. But you go if you want to. I'm too happy to
leave here, but I'll be fine on my own."

I went, for a hideously expensive, uncomfortable, glorious four days. I remember mostly the Acropolis, incredibly more wonderful than its photographs, and my
ungraciousness in declining an invitation to a reception
at the Canadian embassy. I have regretted that gaucherie

ever since. Pam McGann was the ambassador's daughter
and one of my recent art students from CTS. She was
wonderfully supportive, finding me a pension (which had
such an overpowering stench of cat that I could hardly
breathe in it, but she couldn't know that), having me to
dinner, and introducing me to a charming girl who
worked for the embassy and helped me to explore. And
I was too shy to face a diplomatic party at which I would
know nobody. Shame on me!

"Athens, March 1: Exhibition Day at CTS, and I'm
missing Ginny. However, the day has had gifts too, a
wonderful hour on the Acropolis this morning enjoying
new Athens from above as well as old Athens. It is a place
that smoothes out wrinkles in a strange way and seems
timeless, so that an hour goes by in a few minutes. I
wonder if it coloured Greek theology that one could lean
over the wall of the Acropolis and watch life going on
down below, as they imagined their gods doing."

Back in St. Tropez, Ginny was having an exhilarating
time depending on her own French, coping with the
mountain of spinach she had apparently ordered from the
greengrocer, and glad to welcome me home. Once we
were together again in St. Tropez, we had a conference
to plan the balance of the year. Of all the places we had
been, where would we most like to return to paint?

We chose to split May between Sussex and East Anglia, to spend most of June at Brixham in Devon and July
in the west of Ireland, with a week in London to recover
after each bout of work and a week squeezed in for the
whole series of history plays, *Richard II* to *Henry V*, in
Stratford. This last was in faith that the standard of *Henry
VIII* would be maintained.

We drove north into winter again. In Paris, at an antique shop near our scruffy little hotel on the Left Bank, I saw in the window a fifteenth-century oak madonna and child, the very carving that I had imagined in the niche in the hall at Fool's Paradise. That niche was originally intended to be a corner cupboard, but while I was building it, the upper space cried out for a piece of sculpture, so I had left it without a door, in waiting. The price of the madonna and child was moderate, even by my frugal standards, about two hundred dollars, but I hadn't enough money with me to buy it then, and we were leaving Paris the next morning. I arranged to send the necessary amount from England, with a generous addition to cover the cost of air express home. I'm afraid I was dealing with a scamp. Months later the statue came by sea freight, packed so carelessly that Eaton's wouldn't have sent it across the city that way. The lovely figure suffered more damage on that trip to Canada than in the five centuries since its creation. But I was able to glue back the hand and arm, repair the fingers, and see her standing serene at last, the Queen of Heaven and of Fool's Paradise.

Our return to England was home-coming in many ways – familiar money, our own language, ground that we had already covered once. We timed it to give us Easter at Canterbury, where we observed the austere-looking and notorious Red Dean wink at one of the little boys in the choir, who grinned widely back at him.

There was a shock waiting for me when we reached the hotel at Rye. I was handed a cablegram: "Don't come home. I am in good hands. Mother." The rest of the day was frantic. Heart attack? Stroke? Paralysis? There were a couple of desperate hours trying to find a telephone. Hotel phones were not acceptable for transatlantic calls. The police were not willing to tie up their line with a private call. At last I found a good-hearted woman who ran a bed-and-breakfast who let me use her phone. I put in a call to Marjorie, who would know where Mother was and what had happened to her, and then sat for an hour with Ginny beside me for moral support, looking at the telephone, at the keyboard of the guest-house, at the tiled roofs outside the windows, at my doodles on the brown envelope, waiting for the call to go through. Marjorie's voice was clear and she sounded reassuring, even while she appalled me by the news she had. I suppose a fall and two crushed vertebrae is better than the stroke I was afraid of, actually much better. But it was her second bout with broken bones in two years. My poor Mother, facing all that slow painful process again.

Marjorie, underestimating Mother's ingenuity and instinct for drama, had arranged that I should hear about the accident by word of mouth from Ralph Bennett, husband of Madeline, one of my Shawnees and a daughter to me, who was due in London in a day's time. I went up to town to meet him and had a full report. He had been to see Mother and found her already over the worst, although still in hospital. He convinced me that I could go on with my year. I was more than willing to be convinced.

This was when Ginny hit her stride in her work. Her paintings of the Sussex Downs were subtle, exciting, rhythmic. She found a mode between realism and abstraction with a sweeping movement that really said the wind through the grasses, and her colour was warm with all the golden light of the early spring.

For me, the month later on in Brixham was the best painting of the year. We lived in a guest-house there in an attic room overlooking the harbour. We could lie in bed in the morning with our early tea and watch the fishing boats passing the outer breakwater, bringing their catch in to the fish market on the other side of the inner harbour. We would hear the bell ring for the beginning of the daily fish auction. Brixham was a tourist centre as well as an active fishing and market town. The quay was crowded with people and gulls. I found the ideal spot for painting on the flat roof of the "Gents," a small cement building on one corner of the quay. It commanded the whole harbour and all the large and small boats that sagged this way and that on their sides when the tide went out, leaving them stranded on a stretch of mud ribboned with little streams. Nobody bothered me up there.

Stratford was more than we had hoped or dreamed. It was the season that young Richard Burton, still in the power of his idealism, was playing Prince Hal in the two parts of *Henry IV* and in *Henry V*. Michael Redgrave was Richard II. Harry Andrews, Barbara Jefford, Rosalind Atkinson, Alan Badel, Robert Hardy, Anthony Quale, Michael Bates, and Edward Atienza were among the superb ensemble. The designer was none other than Tanya Moiseiwitsch, whose name was new to us then.

When we were in Holland, Goyo had lent us a book about Ireland that spoke enthusiastically about a small hotel on Achill Island, an area that had excited us when

we were driving north from Connemara. We wrote asking if there was a room with a sea view large enough for
two artists to share. The owner's answer assured us that
there was one such, but only one, the other rooms being
no more than "mousetraps." We booked it at once, convinced that anyone who could be so frank to prospective
clients must be a rare and kindred soul. So she proved to
be, with a perceptiveness and tact that chose for us table
companions who in two weeks became friends for the rest
of our lives.

One memorable Irish encounter was with a friend of
hers, a young woman recently widowed, who was trying
to raise her two small sons by working the pocket-hand-
kerchief fields her husband had left her. We were bid to
dinner one night, with the explanation that the roast of
lamb wouldn't keep any longer. She and the little boys
lived in a two-room croft with an earth floor. Brenda
cooked on an open fire on the floor, but her wind-up
gramophone wheezed out classical music and opera, and
she had original paintings of quality on her wall and could
talk with assurance about the European masterpieces we
had just been seeing. Her poverty was not of the spirit.

We were in Ireland when the steamship company
wrote to tell us that our return passage was to be delayed
by three days. Our first reaction was dismay; that would
get us home with hardly a weekend before we were due
back teaching. Then we realized that it was giving us
three unexpected extra days in England. Stratford again!
And indeed we did end our wonderful year with perfor-
mances of *Richard II* and the two parts of *Henry IV*. We had
three halcyon days staying again at the little country inn
with the mother cat and kittens, caught up every evening

in the magic of drama and poetry. We came out of the theatre after the last play to the shocked realization that it was all over. The drive north to Glasgow for embarkation was a funeral procession. This time it was I who succumbed to border-crossing with a bad attack of nervous indigestion, in pain until I managed to persuade the night porter to find me some sodium bicarb. He produced a cupful of it, which gave us the only laugh of the day.

Ginny and I could not stop the tears as we stood in the bow of the ship and felt it moving away from the dock and starting down the Clyde towards the sea and away from adventure and freedom. The elderly Scottish woman standing alone beside us was wiping her eyes too. We put our arms around her and heard that she had been home to Scotland for a last visit and was now on her way back to New Zealand, where she had lived out her marriage and widowhood. We became a threesome for the voyage.

The welcoming party who met us at the Danforth station when we got off the train admitted later that they hardly knew us. Twenty extra pounds do make a difference. All that wonderful French bread and butter. Ginny would never be slim again, and I had to struggle for years to recover, but it was a small price to pay for such a year.

2

The Long Stretch

WE PLUNGED BACK into the discipline of teaching, back into the black tunnel, with the years ahead stretching into dim distance, the way lightened at first by reliving week by week our adventures, sharing the memories. Ginny's students discovered to their delight that an apparently innocent question was apt to set her off into a twenty-minute diversion. My history of art classes had new vitality.

Central Technical School had been built in the prosperous period before the Great War of 1914. It was a fine pseudo-Gothic building of cut stone, accommodating well over two thousand students, of whom about two hundred were in the art department. Some of the art students, in what we called the A classes, came directly out of elementary school and were given their high-school academic work along with a sound basic art education. The B stream was made up of young adults who had finished high school and came for three years of concentrated art study. In both streams we stressed creativity as well as technical competence. They were all taught drawing and painting, lettering and design, sculpture, and illustration, in ways that we hoped would develop the imagination and encourage them to become artists. The various optional subjects offered depended more on the teacher's current enthusiasms than on rigid curricula. Peter Haworth, head of the department, realized that an instructor's excitement about a subject was more important than the name of the course. Whatever problems we chose to assign would involve drawing, design, handling of colour or tone, and respect for material. We wanted to produce artists who had not only the basic skills but enthusiasm and dedication.

As well as these full-time students we had part-time classes for adults who came in for pottery, weaving, metalwork, or drawing and painting from still life or from the model. These classes offered a great refuge for women whose husbands had recently retired, or sometimes for the husbands. The Central Tech pottery students enjoyed a continent-wide reputation and won top prizes in all the competitions.

And there were the adolescents from other departments who were given art for a couple of hours a week in the hope that it would be a civilizing influence. Occasionally we made discoveries of talent in those classes and fought to get the students transferred to the art department, with some notable successes. Joyce Wieland was one so rescued who still thanks us for it. Jack Kuper was another. Harry Klunder was turned away by the main office as underqualified for our courses, but we recognized his talent and argued down the rules.

The school had weathered the depression of the thirties, but twenty-four-hour use during its years of war-emergency classes had left it tired and shabby, showing its age. The federal government decided to provide the funds to clean it up after its long and honourable service.

The walls of the art department were all of natural cedar, ideal for pushing in thumbtacks and pulling them out again, but dark, and darker still after forty years. Peter Haworth ordered them to be painted in pale grey and sunny yellow. At first I felt some regret at losing the warmth of the natural brown wood, but suddenly the physical surroundings were bright and cheerful. Even more welcome were the new fluorescent lights. For the first time it was possible to see what you were doing on the side of the room away from the windows, where previously the light had tested at one candlepower. The greatest boon of all was the reordering of the ventilation system in the art department. Through some combination of ducts and fans, my room, the central one in the corridor that cut across the school above the auditorium, had always acted as the foul-air outlet for the gym. I had taught for seventeen years breathing the ripe stench of sweat and feet. It was not that I had never complained. Engineers came regularly and listened to me and took air samples and vanished defeated. Night after night I drove home across the city unable to get the smell out of my nose. But no more. The miracle was accomplished.

And I was invited to design the cupboards and still-life stands that I yearned for. Until then I had set up arrangements of books, bottles, pots, fruit, or whatever on a wooden drawing-board balanced on a stool. The background of drapery was hung from another drawing-board standing on its edge, held in place by thin braces tacked to the sides of the first. Please Do Not Disturb signs did what they could, but the room was used day and night. Students are human, and adolescents are notoriously clumsy even when not careless. The day that the carpenters brought in my new long counters with permanently fixed backs, some low enough to let the students look down on their subject, some higher, all with neat cupboards below for storing my hoard of draperies and still-life materials, I felt as if I had died and gone to heaven. From then on I loved my room, and took pride in the variety and interest of the arrangements that I could now set up with some sense of security. It still irked me to look out to three other brick walls, but inside the room the views were charming.

The year I returned to teaching I was more active than ever as an exhibiting artist. Ginny and I had a joint showing of our work at Eaton's College Street. The art gallery there had prestige in those days, and this marked for us a step up. We had a second joint exhibition in Woodsworth House and later at Victoria College. That first year after my return I had six solo shows, in Niagara Falls, at Port Colborne, at Pickering College in Newmarket, at St. Nicholas Church in Scarborough, one in Brantford, and another at the head office of British American Oil in Toronto. Besides this I was in nine group shows organized by the art societies or by out-of-town galleries, some of these travelling, and showing in such diverse places as Montreal, New York, London, Ont., Windsor, Sarnia, Hamilton, and Barbados.

There were still very few commercial galleries in Toronto, and only Roberts Gallery showed much Canadian work. Douglas Duncan was operating Picture Loan as an art gallery and rental business, but Ab Isaacs was four years away from opening his first gallery on Gerrard Street. It was a small art scene.

Yet if there was little commercial action, there was a growing appetite for Canadian art in the colleges, universities, and small communities. There were usually more than twenty occasions every year for which I had to choose the entries, frame them, then deliver or crate and ship them. Sunday afternoons were spent dragging paintings from the racks, making the difficult decisions about which ones to send, laying them out on the floor, and, working on my knees, taking the nails out of the frames that had just come back from Windsor and fitting in the new paintings that were to go to Montreal. Sometimes it involved cutting mats as well. Always there were labels, entry forms to fill out or lists to make, and my own records to keep. Sometimes an exhibition would result in a sale, and that would help to pay for the frames and the shipping. Frames were expensive and had to be retouched if they came home damaged, and were used and reused.

I was becoming well known as an artist and teacher, invited to serve on juries and to make speeches at the openings of district exhibitions. I was elected an associate of the Royal Canadian Academy and shortly afterwards a member of the Canadian Society of Painters in Water Colour. Membership in the professional societies was a coveted honour, achieved only after being accepted consistently by their juries and then elected by the membership.

The Water Colour Society quickly conned me into becoming its secretary, unpaid of course, but nevertheless rewarded. One of the rewards was getting to know that outstanding artist Jock Macdonald, the president of the society and a dear man, gentle, thoughtful, unselfish, and with vision. I wished I had been lucky enough to have him as a teacher. Another was contact by mail if not in person with a lively creative group of artists across the country, and the opportunity to gain some sense of the broad picture of water-colour painting in Canada.

Most of the staff of the art department were members of the societies. Peter Haworth and his wife Bobs, Carl Schaefer, Dawson and Kathleen Kennedy, and Charles Goldhamer had all been members and officers. Virginia and Don Neddeau were soon to be elected. The Haworths and Carl were also part of the Canadian Group of Painters, which had developed from the Group of Seven.

This was an association of some of those artists who felt themselves to be the new avant-garde, sympathetic to the pioneering spirit of the Group of Seven but working in more modern ways. Lawren Harris's landscapes had given way to geometric abstractions, and Bert Brooker was experimenting with cubism. The Canadian Group shows were by invitation, not by jury, and as a younger artist I was flattered to be invited to show with them once or twice. Two other of their members, Isabel McLaughlin and Yvonne McKague Housser, both fine artists, began to join us on the long weekend at Thanksgiving and the week at Easter to paint with us up in Haliburton. Yvonne was already one of my favourite people, having taught me at the Ontario College of Art, and Isabel was a year ahead of me there, one of the 1926 sketching party at Kitchener, at which Yvonne had been our resident instructor. Isabel is forever memorable to me as our hostess the next summer on her father's yacht, where I met my first-ever cocktail.

The Haliburton painting weekends and Easter holidays were great parties and stimulating for the work itself, for the gatherings in the Haworth room in the motel for a survey of the day's achievements, and for the provocative questions our friend Herman Voaden, who came over from his cottage to join us for dinner, would fling at us to start a discussion. But our most solid work sessions were in the summer, when the same members of the art staff, along with Kath and Dawson Kennedy, friends Nancy Caudle and Flo Smedley, and sometimes my brother Douglas and his wife Audrey and son Dale, would be down on the Gaspé coast together, staying at Liza Jean's boarding house at Corner of the Beach.

Nancy Caudle was a friend dating from high-school days at Malvern Collegiate, still living in the Beach area of Toronto and a close associate of mine at St. Aidan's Church. Her drawings for the high-school year-book had been my inspiration before I was ever an art student, but family responsibilities had forced her into commercial art and kept her there. Through her I had met Florence Smedley, who had moved up from St. Lambert in Quebec to become part of our inner circle of friends at St. Aidan's. They had been joyfully adopted as fellow artists ever since the three of us had shared a memorable painting trip with the Haworths at Cap-à-l'Aigle just after the war. They had earned for themselves a welcome in our gang any time, any place.

The years painting on the Gaspé coast were wonderful periods of renewal and mutual inspiration and stimulus. Although we lived together at Corner of the Beach, we went off in twos or threes to paint at Barachois or any other of the fishing villages within a twenty-mile range, and brought back the day's work for mutual appreciation and criticism. Those Gaspé summers further cemented the fellowship of the staff of the art department.

Anne Cameron, inspector of the teaching of art for our part of the educational system, was a person we liked and respected. She came to us in what we considered a suitable spirit of humility, to get ideas and to see what art education at its best could be. (I have never heard her version, which might be quite different.) One day she rounded up Charles, Dawson, Ginny, and me and advised us strongly to take the summer courses at the Ontario College of Education that would qualify us as specialists, eligible for positions as assistants or full heads of departments. Peter was approaching retirement age, and we were running the risk of having someone from outside put in over us. That warning did it. All four of us signed up, feeling that if we were in it together, it might be at least bearable.

It was a travesty of education. One of the compulsory subjects was English. Although to qualify for the course you had to be judged a superior teacher by your principal and inspector, the first day was spent teaching the class how to address a business letter. Having been a successful secretary of a national organization for two years, I was not amused. In a spirit of mischief Dawson asked the lecturer what he thought of the word "irregardless," and was answered, "Well, it's *used*." I was appalled at the prospect of seeing my whole five weeks so wasted, and managed to bow out of that class by explaining to the professor privately that what I really needed was time for library research on the art of the Byzantine empire and that I would be happy to write a report on the subject. I made good use of those hours for specialized study every morning.

For two hot summers we sat through boring and useless lectures and seminars, consoled inadequately by one good course in economics, which was well taught and new to all of us. The only other consolation was the fun we had together over our egg sandwiches and milkshakes at the Varsity Restaurant before going our separate ways. One sweet memory. At the end of one of our courses there was a really mean examination paper with trivial but tricky questions. Meeting the professor on our way out, Charlie greeted him with, "Is there something wrong with your home life?"

We were all given specialist standing and had the satisfaction of seeing our pay-cheques jump, but I never did receive an answer to the carefully worded, tactful letter I wrote making suggestions about how such courses in the future could be made more valuable to the individual and to the system.

One of my constructive suggestions was to give the teachers an experience of Canada's Stratford. The miracle that we had seen in England had come to Ontario. From the moment of the first news reports of the plans for a Shakespearean festival, Ginny and I were agog with excitement. We passed the contagion to Nan and Flo, and we four were there on the very first night in the tent in 1953. We will never forget the opening image as the lights went up, Alec Guinness, Richard III, perched on the balcony, one leg over the edge, his red cloak hanging almost to the floor, and his voice, his matchless voice, "Now is the winter of our discontent / Made glorious summer by this sun of York." Stratford has become for me the high spot of the year, shared by the same three friends for thirty seasons, until Flo's failing health kept her home.

In 1956, when I was newly elected president of the Canadian Society of Painters in Water Colour, Tom Patterson, who first dreamed the festival and did so much to make the dream come true, was the VIP who opened the exhibition for us at the Art Gallery of Ontario. It was a proud moment for me to be on the platform with him. I cherish the photograph of Tom presenting the CSPWC award for best painting in the show to Tom Hodgson, one of my old students and eventually one of the Painters Eleven, while I beam at both of them. The red brocade evening dress that I was wearing, made specially for the occasion, is still very often brought out and worn at Christmastime, with some satisfaction that I have actually taken in the seams.

That was just before the societies were jockeyed out of the Art Gallery of Ontario. The next annual juried exhibition of the society during my presidency was hung in the Hamilton Art Gallery, with another great figure, this one new to the Canadian scene, as our guest. Dr. Boyd Neel, whose Boyd Neel Orchestra had made musical history in England in recovering the baroque repertoire for concert-goers, was the newly appointed dean of the faculty of music at the University of Toronto. I called for him at his home and drove him out to the Sheepfold for dinner, and eventually to Hamilton for the opening.

The Sheepfold, a gracious old farmhouse near Streetsville, was already the setting for the best parties of the Central Tech gang. Jocelyn Taylor, our new colleague in the art department, lived there with Polly Harris and George McMurtry, an old family friend who had come the weekend they moved in to help them settle, and never left. The Sheepfold had fields, a creek, giant trees, and Canadian art crowding the walls. Boyd, tall, balding, urbane, was charming and charmed, and his pleasure spilled over to me to become the beginning of a friendship that lasted until his death.

It was that spring that Peter retired. Charles Goldhamer, senior among us senior teachers, succeeded him as head of the department, but Peter and Bobs were still very much part of our world. The Sheepfold parties were better than ever because they became reunions. Peter was elected president of the Ontario Society of Artists and chaired our meetings; both Peter and Bobs were always with us at Haliburton and on the Gaspé.

I found Charlie to be a good director, willing to listen, and his added responsibilities gave me more senior painting classes. Graham Gore became the new principal of the school, eager to use the art department to enhance the school's reputation. The demands were heavy, but we had an exhilarating sense of working together as a team and being appreciated by the students and by the administration.

I began to feel unequal to the pressure and realized that I was not well, tired all the time, weak and hollow for no apparent reason, having to drag myself about. Dr. Found was a friend as well as my doctor, elderly and experienced. He asked me how old I was and told me that it was menopause starting, and then entertained me with stories of the bizarre symptoms that some of his other (nameless) patients had exhibited. He also gave me a shot of vitamin B to relieve my immediate misery, and I left, shocked but comforted to know that there was some reason for my malaise and that I would probably recover in time. That was when I reminded myself that life begins at forty, and was tempted to add bitterly that it lasts about four years.

"July 13, 1956: It's a shame that I haven't written since last summer. It isn't that I'm not living all year. It's really that the days are *too* full – there's just no leisure to put things down. 1. This has been the year that I rebelled against the teaching load and tried to cut down to four days a week. No dice. 2. Charlie's being director meant a basic release from tension, but the pace picked up and there were *no* intervals all year, no spares, hardly an easy class in a whole week, two classes of boys who were not art students, and a double class at the museum on Friday afternoon."

Marjorie was living in Birchcliff, a possible route between Central Tech and Fool's Paradise. Two or three times a week I could get a cup of tea and a few minutes with her on my way home. These were the years when there were always toys on the floor, chaos in the kitchen, and small children between us physically, if not metaphorically. But Marjorie involved the children in her welcome so that they grew up conditioned to believe that my arrival was a great event. And once in a while she organized a weekend when one of them would be sent home with me to be my company until Sunday afternoon, when the whole family would arrive with a picnic supper for us all. Sometimes I felt that I didn't have time for this extra complication in my hectic life, but I realized that Marjorie was making sure that I knew her treasures and that they knew me. Thanks to her they became my children too, and are my treasures now.

Mother was in a small house not far from the Wood ménage. Roy was very good to her, doing the man's chores around her house and occasionally collecting her in the car to share in their family dinners. The children learned to accept her and let the stories that she had told too often roll over their heads. Margaret Doris, Marjorie's second daughter, used to cut Mother's lawn when she was about twelve, and tells me now that she developed her resilience under criticism from contact with my mother. Marjorie taught the children to anticipate Mother's acerbity and laughed about it with them, so that they found it amusing instead of hurtful.

Mother spent many Sundays with me, sitting with her embroidery, making one of the big cut-work tablecloths that were her pleasure. My friends enjoyed her, and providing we were not left too long dependent on our own conversation, we got along very well. Even over the telephone it was hard for us to talk for many minutes without finding ourselves in disagreement about something. The only genuinely mutual enthusiasm we had was for my cats, so if we found ourselves arguing, Mother would say, "How are the cats?" and restore peace.

Tammy was a beautiful Persian tabby, affectionate, but with no sense of humour. Her litter-mate was a short-haired black tom, whom I named Nick because he was full of the old, but who was not only mischievous but loving, the most loving creature I have ever met. My first year in residence at Fool's Paradise was an education in mice, and after everyone had advised me to get a cat, I did reluctantly accept these two kittens, small enough to carry about on one hand. The first thing they did for me was to free me from any uneasiness about mysterious noises in the night. From then on I assumed that any disturbance I heard was made by the kittens, and nothing to be alarmed about. The first week I had them a strange car did come up the drive one night and ended up stuck in the soft clay of the flower-beds on the lawn. I was so protective of the kittens that I felt nothing but indignation, and found courage to give the drunks in the car a good scolding for their carelessness.

When the kittens were young they were inseparable, playing and sleeping together. But one day when they were almost full-grown, Nick disappeared. Tammy and I were concerned, then anxious, and finally, as dusk fell and still no Nick, we were both upset. We walked the field together, calling. However, it was not from the field that he appeared but up over the edge of the ravine, and he came paying no attention to us at all. He swaggered – there is no other word for it – as he made for his supper dish. I could see in my mind's eye the cigarette hanging from the side of his lip, and his cap on backwards. While he wolfed down his food, Tammy had a good sniff at him, spat her disgust, and from that time on had never a civil word for him. Nick would tease her, raising his paw as if ready to attack, while she cowered in a corner in a paroxysm of rage. I suspect she knew he would never touch her.

In spite of its auspicious beginning, Nick had little satisfaction in his sex life. He never refused a fight, and never won one. Time after time he would limp home wounded, and after the cuts or scratches became infected he would have to have his leg soaked in hot water. He learned to put his own foot in the basin. I dreaded an operation that might change his personality, but finally for his own protection I had him neutered. There was no change in him. As before, he wanted to be with me whatever I was doing, so that I learned to do housework wearing him on my shoulder, and to sleep with one of the cats on each side of me.

A gift from England was the Croggon family. Madeleine came with an introduction from Kay Hilken, who had been a friend since my first year at art school, and when I invited Madeleine out for a day at Fool's Paradise, she asked if she might bring along her young brother. We three were at home with each other at once. Malcolm was a young man just out of the navy, intelligent and witty. Madeleine was two or three years older, an artist by training and instinct, sharing her brother's wit, a delightful companion. Shortly after her arrival here she put herself through university to become an occupational therapist. This work took her to Kingston and then to Ottawa, where she married. She lived for a while in a corner of an old furniture mill, and was inspired by the fascinating odd shapes that appeared among the discarded scraps of wood to start on the wood collages that are among her most original and satisfying works. Malcolm, left in Toronto, became my friend, my theatre-and-concert companion, my co-woodsman for the annual fall clean-up, and my barman and right-hand man at party time. He was wiry and athletic, a keen tennis player, but music was his first love. I used to marvel to hear Malcolm talking to Boyd Neel about music, and able to hold his ground.

Malcolm and Boyd Neel and Barbara Greene were the guests at one of my most memorable dinner parties. Barbara, a water-colourist, was a colleague in the art department and my neighbour on the bluffs. There were just the four of us. Dinner was under control, either in the oven or in the refrigerator. After the usual walk through the woods and down to the edge of the bluffs to look at the lake, we gathered at the fireplace with our drinks in our hands. It was cool enough for a fire, but the draught was balky and I had trouble with the lever that is supposed to open it. "Oh no," I thought, "not something else breaking down!" A second try seemed to dislodge whatever was blocking the damper, and I lit a match. It was a well-laid fire, bursting promptly into flame. But there were noises in the chimney, and I wondered if perhaps the soot was catching fire. More noises, and down into the fire dropped a cat, surrounded by little tongues of flame like the Holy Ghost.

All four of us leapt into action. Somebody grabbed the fire screen and pulled it forward. Someone else dashed after the cat, who had jumped at a window and was clawing his way up the curtain. Malcolm opened the door to the porch and garden, and we watched the brown woolly creature streak across the grass and vanish into the shrubbery. It was a great relief to see my own cats strolling into the living-room curious to know what the excitement was all about.

The next day, up at the hardware store buying wire

mesh for the chimney so that it could never happen again, I heard that a child had reported her cat's having been "thrown into the fire" by some fiend. I went to offer an apologetic explanation to the owner and make a sick call on the cat now that I had discovered where he lived. The patient was not at home, having recovered and gone about his business, but I was amused to be told that he was an orange Persian. Not when I saw him he wasn't.

When I returned from my first year of study in England in 1936, the rector of St. Aidan's, my old friend Dr. Cotton, had persuaded me to assist his new curate with the reorganization of the Sunday school. Dr. Basil English, "the Doc" to Nancy and Flo and me, became our friend. He was a teacher of rare scholarship, an amusing companion, and a visionary who attracted many teenagers, both boys and girls, to share and work for that vision. He had an eye, and I appreciated how he used Nancy and me and his other artists when there were visual decisions to be made. In the 1950s St. Aidan's was a very conservative parish, and the Doc had to introduce changes slowly and cautiously.

At his invitation Nan and I developed the Christmas Nativity play at St. Aidan's, with him as our narrator. Unlike the production at the Church of the Holy Trinity in downtown Toronto, ours allowed the characters in the story to speak their own parts and used the Doc's wonderful voice to link the scenes together. What we tried to do was glorious, and the drama we saw in our imagination is more vivid to me now than the drama we actually achieved. We had an elderly but enthusiastic amateur electrician in the congregation who figured out a way of hanging a light, high above the action, that would be invisible until the three Magi came in their procession up the centre aisle, when it would start to glow, becoming brighter as they approached Bethlehem. This was kept as a surprise for the director. A second surprise, which I am still trying to forgive, was the projection on the wall of the sanctuary at the climax of the play of a sentimental slide of Christ in Gethsemane. How do you explain to an old boy, without hurting his feelings, that a director doesn't like surprises?

It was at one of the Nativity plays that the Doc muffed his lines, got mixed up in the scenes, and needed prompting. Not long afterwards we realized that this was an early symptom of an illness that was progressive and would be fatal. It was a bitter irony that the friend with the most acute mind and the least tolerance of stupidity should be stricken with a brain disease.

The parish was left for a while to the ministry of two young men. Hugh Stiff, who had been the curate, was named priest in charge. To assist him he enlisted the part-time services of a classmate, the Reverend Brian Freeland, who was working for the Canadian Broadcasting Corporation. Both these men were to mature into strong leaders. Hugh Stiff became a bishop, and finally dean of Toronto. Brian Freeland became director of religious broadcasting for the CBC while continuing as an active parish priest and a promoter of all the arts as the work of God. Together they were responsible for a lively church in the months before we were given a permanent rector. Nan and I felt like part of a great team.

Perhaps that is what started me designing a drastic new

look for the chancel of the church. I began to imagine it
hung on either side with an avenue of glorious banners
that would lead the eye back to the altar. This was the
Henry VII chapel at Westminster speaking to me. They
could be movable, so that the two front banners would
celebrate the current season of the church year and be
moved further back as the year progressed and the new
season's images became appropriate.

I waited until Canon Snell was established as rector in
1956 before broaching the subject of banners to him or
the advisory board. The members of the board had misgivings, but they agreed, after seeing my sketch of the
whole plan and my full-size mock-up of one of the banners, to let me make and hang two on a trial basis before
authorizing the whole project.

Making these two was a labour of love occupying many
happy months, shopping for fabrics, finding and buying
the right material for a strong background, choosing
colours that would show up well against each other,
discovering fine leather-backed gold leaf for touches of
brilliance. My ceiling at Fool's Paradise had tie-beams
high enough to let me hang the full ten feet of banner and
see it all at once with the design elements pinned in place
for revision and refining. I have never felt more conviction about a job, or understood better Dorothy L. Sayers's
words, "You never make a fundamental mistake about the
things that really matter." I found patience I did not know
I had, and the willingness to change, to prune, to correct,
to scrap. I began to understand the terrible ruthlessness
of creative love.

The stitching was pure pleasure, watching the work

grow under my fingers with the difficult decisions all made. Finally I invented a hanging device for hoisting the banners into place and changing them readily, and hired a carpenter to bring his high ladders and mount the necessary hooks in the chancel ceiling. All was ready in time for the sixtieth anniversary of the church, and the photographs taken at the big gala service on Anniversary Sunday in 1957 show the first pair hanging in their glory.

When I came to the early service the next Sunday morning, they had vanished, and their hooks with them. I was speechless with shock. I skip the weeks in which I wrestled with my sense of personal injury, my indignation that the promised review was never made, my anger that I was treated with such contempt and my work not valued, and my temptation to leave the church in pique. I prayed for grace to forgive, and came at last to see the humour of the affair when I learned that the pillar whose influence had removed the banners was a man whose front lawn was adorned with plaster gnomes.

It was some small sop to my pride that the Trinity banner eventually found a home in St. James' Cathedral and that my own church now has the panel of St. Aidan hanging high in the narthex.

I needed to get away and forget all about it, and had for some time been feeling the need of a change of territory for painting. I persuaded Flo Smedley to come with me to England in the summer of 1958. It meant that we missed Nan's wedding to Ken Wright, but she was ac-quiring not only a husband but three children and a wide

family connection and didn't need us there. Kath and
Dawson Kennedy turned up while we were overseas that
summer and joined us to make a good foursome.

We were staying in a pub near Whitby in Yorkshire,
notable for a rather brassy blonde hostess who helped her
husband run the place and was seldom seen without two
large poodles, the bitch as friendly as her mistress, the
male distinctly cool to strangers. The vicar of the little
parish where Flo and I found an early service to suit us
had once visited Vancouver, and was interested in these
Canadians who had appeared in his church. When we
came home from painting on Monday afternoon, there
was a message for me to phone him, and I was invited to
use the telephone in the manager's office, with apologies
that I would have to share the office with the male poodle,
who was shut in there because the female had come into
heat. I didn't mind, and while I talked to the vicar, who
was inviting all four of us to his home to see his Canadian
slides, I was tickling the poodle's ears and rubbing the
back of his neck and having my hand licked. When I went
to thank the manager for the use of his room, I exclaimed,
"He gets quite chummy when you're alone with him." It
was the sudden blank on the publican's face that told me
he thought I was talking about the vicar.

The best part of that evening was the walk home. It
had been a typical showing of amateur travel snapshots,
the boredom enlivened only by a rather hot little argu-
ment that arose when Dawson disputed the vicar's
sweeping dismissal of the Americans' participation in the
war against Hitler as meagre and useless. Dawson was
outraged and countered with a list of some of the States'

major contributions. It was none too soon when tea put an end to that discussion. Kath and I led the walk home, and we heard Dawson behind us, "God damn it. God *damn* it!" We swung back. "What's the matter?" we asked. Dawson was shaking his head in disgust. "Did you hear me defending those bloody Americans?"

Farther north we found good painting near Wark-on-Tyne, and I did the Birtley churchyard that is now in the permanent collection of the Art Gallery of Ontario. We also found Hexham Abbey and went there on a Sunday morning for a civic service. The mayor was a Chaucerian figure in gold chain, beard, and business suit. The choir-boys were an assortment of well-behaved children, some with the raw bones and extended ears of the Northumbrian farmer, one a pretty little boy, dark hair, red cheeks, small perfect mouth. I kept looking for the men they would grow into. In his sermon the rector shocked us with references to "the crisis," the emergency we had been living with all week, etc., asking sternly how many people had spent as much time in prayer as in reading the newspaper and listening to the news. All very alarming. He was talking to four people who had been in plenty of churches and services but had been hearing no news. After church Dawson went streaking across the square in search of a paper. It was the Suez crisis, a confrontation between Britain and Egypt, with the United States declining to back Britain – serious enough, and Anthony Eden had just resigned as foreign minister.

Our third painting-ground that summer was on Holy Island, or Lindisfarne, just off the Northumbrian coast, where St. Aidan came in the sixth century to Christianize the heathen Norse invaders. It is a peninsula that is cut off by the sea at high tide and becomes an island. Its insularity is one of its greatest charms, jealously protected. The residents take very lightly the rules that govern the mainland. Closing time at the three pubs is less than rigid, and since nobody on Holy Island is willing to accommodate a resident constable, the level of sociability is high. But one night the telephone rang at the pub where we were enjoying the local brew and the publican flicked the lights with a stern "Drink up, ladies and gentlemen. Closing, please." Word had come that a bobby was on his way over the causeway, and by the time we were out of the darkened pub and along as far as the square, there he was, sitting on his motorcycle, responding cheerfully to the greetings from three streams of strollers whose way home lay through the square. A conviction for late closing would mean loss of licence, and nobody, including the bobby, really wanted that.

It was at Holy Island that I heard the news, worse to me than the Suez crisis, that my dear Nicky had been lost for a week and, when found, was said by the vet to have had a stroke, which had left him paralysed, unable to crawl home out of the rain, with the result that he had almost died of pneumonia. He was now safe at home, trying to walk but staggering pitifully. My friends Margaret Cork and Gwen Oliver, who were living at Fool's Paradise for the summer, would nurse him and not have him put down until I came home. Bless Marg and Gwen for their loving care of the little guy. He was still pretty unsteady when I first saw him, but he gradually made a complete recovery and lived for another nine years after that, the nine best years of his life.

In the spring of 1959 I began to be homesick for northern Ontario and to yearn for a summer cottage again. It was more than twenty-five years since Ethel Curry and I had lived together in a hunting shack at North Lake. The rented cottage on Silver Island in Muskoka, where Marjorie and I had been so happy as children, and the McCarthy cabin at Beaumaris had provided a very different way of life from the motels, guest-houses, and hotels that Ginny and I had shared with our friends at Haliburton and the Gaspé. While I was talking to Marjorie about this one afternoon, perched on the stool in her kitchen and sipping tea, she reminded me that Marg and Gwen had once rented a cottage on Georgian Bay that they had learned of through Yvonne Williams. Yvonne was a stained-glass artist who had graduated with the Governor General's medal the year before I started at the art college, and whom I knew through our many mutual friends. I phoned her and she brought a box of slides to school to let us see the rocks, the pools lying in them, the sparkling bay with its islands. Ginny and I were charmed and wasted no time in booking the cottage for a couple of weeks in August and persuading our Sheepfold friends to rent a second cottage near it. Marjorie's daughter, Margaret Doris, was sixteen that summer and was to be there with us so that Marjorie and Roy could go on their first trip together overseas with easy minds.

It was a case of love at first sight. The track over rock outcroppings and through juniper bushes to get to the door was high adventure, and promised the privacy that we craved. The cottage itself was a single large room, built of stone up to window level, with half-logs set vertically above the stone. The end towards the bay was window

on three sides, looking across a breast of rock to the water
and to a pink granite island that lay beyond like a half-
submerged giant with a placid smile where a cleft in the
rock crossed his face. Gulls rested on him, and a Caspian
tern who usually appropriated the highest point. With the
Sheepfold friends next door we became a busy artists'
colony. Like the rest of us Polly Harris went sketching
every day, but she seldom went farther than the shallow
pond between the two cottages, full of singing frogs and
washed by the waves when a launch passed. To this day
we call it Polly's Puddle. Margaret looked after us, and
became part of us and of the place in those few short
weeks.

When we left, Marg and Gwen followed as the next
tenants. They reported by mail that the two cottages were
to be sold and that a business magnate from Pittsburgh
had been around looking them over. None of us could
afford to buy them or even one of them, but we agreed,
after much conference by letter and telephone, to go into
partnership – Yvonne, Ginny, Doris, and Marg-and-
Gwen as one would buy both of them, and keep the sweet
seclusion that we had found so good. We gathered there,
all five of us, over Labour Day weekend to celebrate the
purchase, and were in the larger cottage, busy tearing out
a partition to open up the living-room, when the owner
called in to see us. It dawned on us with some horror that
no money had yet passed hands and we didn't actually
own the place, but it appeared, as we shared a hastily
made cup of tea, that to him as to us our word was enough.
On the road out to the highway after that memorable
weekend, there were five bluebirds perched on a wire. I
remembered the bluebird on the stake that had marked

the site of the house at Fool's Paradise almost twenty
years earlier, and knew that no omen could have been
better.

Mother was too frail that autumn for me to take her up
to see the cottage, although I knew that the rocks and
islands would have reminded her of the summers at Baie
Fine, and she would have loved the place. She had had a
severe heart attack in the spring, so severe that neither
the ambulance boys nor the nurse who admitted her to
St. Michael's Hospital thought she could pull through. I
realized this when I saw the look on the nurse's face as I
offered her Mother's slippers and gown.

I have thought since that Mother should have died in
that attack. The next year she was not really living,
although she stayed stubbornly on in her own home with
Meals on Wheels and dinners from a local restaurant as
an alternative. But her zest was gone.

That spring I added on to Fool's Paradise the large
studio that my work was crying for. Mr. Janes agreed to
be my builder, although reluctantly. He was the carpenter
who had made such a beautiful job of the original house
and had gone on to become a contractor as well as
carpenter. I had recommended him for two houses, including the new rectory for St. Aidan's, which I had
designed, and they were both beautifully crafted. But
Roy Nurse, who was the churchwarden in charge of the
construction of the rectory, recognized Mr. Janes's profound distrust of women as well as the advisory board's
distrust of me, and conspired to keep my finger in that pie
well hidden.

I found it amusing to see the change in the old man's attitude as the work on the studio progressed. At first he was very cool. "How do ye wish me to do this?" "What would ye be planning to line this with?" But as the building went on, he began to like it and changed his tune. "Ye wouldn't want anything but good pine here." "We'd better use the same on the ceiling as on the walls." Our only unpleasantness was the day I spoke to the roofer about something and received a proper bawling out. "You speak to me and I'll speak to the roofer," he stormed, quite correctly, of course. He was all over the scaffolding, up at the cathedral ceiling, outside on the roof. I could hardly believe it when I was told a year later, when a stroke put him into hospital, that he was eighty-nine years old at the time.

At school I was creating an impressive library of slides to use in teaching the history of art. During my year travelling with Ginny I had bought excellent postcards of architecture and sculpture, and had then borrowed from the library good books with beautiful photographs that could be copied on to slides. But there were gaps, and I began to think that I should plan another year of travelling to let me visit and record the Byzantine art that I had learned about at summer school. I wanted to see Egypt with my own eyes. And it would be a chance to stay with friends in New Zealand and do some painting. Ginny said a regretful but firm no, so I would have to go on my own.

This was the only time I ever approached the Canada Council for help. Ten years' teaching with the Toronto Board of Education entitled me to a sabbatical year on half-salary, but that was not enough to accomplish the amount of travel I needed for my purposes. I was eligible for a senior fellowship that would take up the slack. I was hopeful that my record as an exhibiting artist and teacher and my work in the professional art societies would earn me this award. I learned better. One of the recipients that year was a man of about my age whose claims to a fellowship were on similar grounds to mine, but in every respect appreciably less.

While I was still pondering ways and means, Mother had another heart attack. It was the night of a Royal Canadian Academy opening at the Art Gallery of Ontario. I was in evening dress, just leaving to pick up Nan, when Mother's neighbour called me. Mother was in pain when I got there, but I helped her to bed and saw her quiet and asleep before I left. I took Nan to the gallery but realized that I could not go on with that part of the program with Mother on my mind, so I left her there with friends and called my brother Doug when I got back to Mother's. He shared my vigil. And he shared my incredulity when, after two or three hours of silence, we began to suspect that perhaps she had died. Did she really feel cool to the touch? We called the doctor, and he confirmed that she was indeed gone. For twenty-five years Mother had been talking about dying, going through dramatic accidents and sustaining serious injuries, having heart attacks that frightened everyone, but she was a survivor and had surprised us all so often with her toughness that we couldn't believe it.

I seem to have successfully blocked out the funeral and the reception afterwards. I do remember one desperate moment when the choir sang something from the *Messiah* and I had to fight to keep my control. And there were some miserable days of drudgery cleaning Mother's little house, and feeling the contrast between her fussy standards of housekeeping and the dirt and neglect that spoke of a frail eighty-three-year-old who no longer had good eyesight. I felt jealous for her pride in her home and unwilling that anyone else should see its shame.

Perhaps neither Doug nor his wife Audrey ever outgrew the threat that Mother posed to them. Although she was generous to them with money, she told all their neighbours how much she was helping them. She never tried to imagine how anyone else felt about anything and had no tenderness for their pride. Doug and Audrey protected young Dale from her asperity, so that he saw very little of her and never knew what a colourful character he had as a grandmother. God knows she was difficult, but I am grateful to have known her.

I think it was the frustrated artist in her that made her love of me so possessive, so that she tried to direct my life in her way. I know that if I had not inherited from both my parents strength enough to make my own decisions in spite of her, I could have become Mother's doormat. And that would not have satisfied either of us. We had our tensions, and six sad years when she would have nothing to do with me. But we had many years afterwards to become friends and for her to learn that an independent daughter is not a bad thing to have as one grows older. Mother gave me the strong constitution, the physical and emotional energy, the organizing capacity, and the love of an audience that are among my most conspicuous gifts. She has left me good memories and many of them. She is unforgettable.

3

Around the World

I WAS VERY GRATEFUL that Mother died before I had to tell her that I was planning another year away. I had been dreading breaking the news to her. Now it wouldn't be necessary, and my share of Mother's estate would provide the money I needed. When Ginny decided that she could not come with me and there was no other companion in sight, much of the glamour faded from the prospect. But my reasons for going were still valid, and I settled down doggedly to make plans. Since my major objectives were outside Britain and Europe, I was plunging into an unknown world, unknown even from reading. Marjorie gave me a fine big coffee-table book, *Asia* by Martin Hurlimann, and I pored over it and noted the location of the most exciting of the sculptures and architecture. I took my memos to a travel agent and with his help worked out an itinerary that would include the best of the sites I had seen in Hurlimann's book and, at the same time, route me through New Zealand to visit friends. It would allow me to spend time in Greece, to see the Holy Land, to photograph Saint Sophia in Istanbul and the dramatic monuments of Egypt. Ginny and Flo would join me in England and travel with me all summer to reward me for the year of solitary wandering.

One of the friends of the pioneer days at Fool's Paradise was "Ginty," Pearl McGinnis, the first-ever school nurse at Central Tech, who came to us after the war and whom we perceived as just one more threat when we found the first lot of health forms in our mailboxes. Not another round of questionnaires! But before the end of the staff meeting at which she was introduced to us, she had us eating out of her hand. She and her friend Milly Bell would come down to Fool's Paradise on a Saturday or Sunday, and they would plant potatoes or hoe the garden or join me in whatever I was doing. Ginty had an instinct for mothering, and she took me on as a daughter or younger sister. When I was planning my sabbatical, to start in June of 1961, I discovered that both Ginty and Milly would be retired by the end of the year and were planning to close up the apartment they had been sharing since Milly's mother had died, to take off in their car for a year of vagabond travel in North America. They were easily persuaded to spend their first year of freedom at Fool's Paradise, keeping home warm for me and loving my cats.

It was that spring of 1961 that dear old Tammy faded away. She had been getting thinner and frailer, and when she made it clear that she had stopped living, I had her put to sleep. Kath and Dawson were cat people, understanding my grief and concerned about my bereavement.

They turned up the next Saturday with a fluffy little
tortoiseshell kitten. I appreciated the kindness of the
thought, but what would Nick think? Would he accept
another cat? He was asleep on the couch in the studio,
and I put the little stranger down beside him, nervously.
He stirred, awoke, looked along to where she was at his
side, then twisted down and began to give her a thorough
bath, which she accepted with loud purrs. From that
moment they were inseparable. He brought her up,
taught her to use the cat door, to hunt, how to kill and eat
her prey, and played with her all the endearing games that
were his trademark.

honesty

It was a mercy that school was so demanding that June.
I was having severe attacks of nerves, feeling panic-
stricken at the prospect of such a long time on my own. I
began to realize how custom supports me normally, how
I was in control because I knew the ropes. My teaching
day was a heavy but familiar routine, from the drive in to
town, knowing just when to change lanes, to my arrival
at the staff parking lot, where there was a place for me.
The shops on the way home, Toronto theatres when I had
a night out, the few restaurants that I visited regularly,
were all like old shoes to me. If I went to a new place in
Toronto, it was with Boyd or Malcolm or someone else
to share the novelty. But in the year I was planning, every
situation would be strange. And I had to think ahead and
carry everything I might need with me, and yet keep my
needs so simple that I was still travelling light.

Marjorie and Roy, with two of their daughters and my
carefully organized luggage, drove me to the Toronto

airport on the last day of June 1961. Because I was far too strung up to be good for anything else, we went early and had a picnic lunch together in a farm field within sight of the airport. I was tense with the prospect of a whole year away from home and the people I loved, but by then it was too late to escape it.

The Woods dropped me and my bags at the departure door and took off on the first leg of their summer trip to New England. I began the routine of checking in, and was advised that my flight to San Francisco was delayed six hours and all my connections would be lost. There was a re-routing possible that would get me there late in the evening instead of in the afternoon. They would notify the Bennetts, who were to come from Palo Alto to meet me.

The next crisis was the discovery in mid-flight that I had no ticket. With the route change I should have obtained a whole new set of documents, and since this was before the check and double-check that precedes boarding these days, I had embarked without them. The flight officer was exasperated and stern. I remembered Peter Haworth and how I had discovered his soft side when I had cried for help because a bat flew into our bedroom at Cap-à-l'Aigle. I became a helpless female, apologetic, innocent, willing to do anything the flight officer should ask me to. He gave up fighting, patted my shoulder, and coped.

I was to stay for the first week with my darling Madeline, the Shawnee who had become like a daughter to me, whose children as they arrived were made my godchildren. She and Ralph had moved out to California, and this trip was a chance to see her on my way to the Far East. Ralph and she had sat for hours waiting for me, and gone home disappointed and worried. When at long last I reached San Francisco and found nobody to meet me, I called them at Palo Alto. They gallantly set out again for the thirty-mile drive north. We met at last and reached home at some hour that for me was the dead of night. So much for the airline's promise to notify my friends.

Saying goodbye to the Bennetts a week later and starting out for Japan was leaving home all over again. This was when the strangeness really began. I flew into heat such as I had never before experienced or imagined. At the airport in Tokyo in the early dawn, while waiting for a taxi to appear, I reorganized my suitcases and got rid of the sweater and jacket that I had been wearing. I had bought in Toronto a two-piece dress with a full skirt and a loose sleeveless top worn outside, collarless but cut close to the neck, cool, modest, comfortable for walking or climbing. With gloves and a soft hat it was formal enough for any situation. A bra and brief panties were enough under it, no slip or stockings required. Then I had copied it in a different printed fabric so that I could wash one set and wear the other. I should have been comfortable.

But not in Tokyo that summer. The international students' hostel where I stayed had no air conditioning. Both temperature and humidity were setting records. I would take a cool bath at night and lie on the bed without even a sheet, hoping to get an hour or two of sleep before I had to get up for another bath to cool me down. On a bus one day I felt what I feared were flies crawling down the back of my leg and discovered to be trickles of perspiration. I hadn't known that the backs of your legs could perspire.

Tokyo at that time had a small concentration of sky-scrapers and big buildings in the district known as the Ginza, and beyond that miles and miles of narrow streets with one-storey unpainted frame buildings, all similar in appearance. One morning I took a bus to the Ginza, and after travelling for what seemed far too long I asked someone, "Ginza?" pointing ahead. "Ginza," repeated the stranger, and pointed behind.

I leapt off the bus at the next stop, but the crowd that quickly gathered around this obvious stranger were as helpless as I. They turned my map upside-down and back again, unable to read it or to locate us on it. They wanted to help. Finally someone summoned a policeman, who couldn't read the map either but who led me back to the police station, where he was able to get a man on the phone who spoke English. He told me where I was and ordered the local constable to escort me to the nearest train and point me in the right direction.

I began to enjoy Japan when I escaped from Tokyo and the unbearable heat on an air-conditioned supertrain to Kyoto. The platform was thronged with friends and relations, who suddenly disappeared as the train started to move. I looked out in alarm and saw that, as one, they were bent double in a low bow. Up again, and again down. It was comic and beautiful.

"Kyoto, July 11, 1961: This afternoon I started off by myself to find the Garden of Stones. I found plenty of gardens, some with stones, but not the famous one. I sat around on one rock after another, avoiding the moss but not the ants, making miserable little drawings, and then went up higher to see what was there. I found an earnest youth, sweet, and so much like students I have known and loved at home, who wanted to practise his English on me. His two friends joined us, and we had a pleasant hour, which included a deliciously funny walk down the road with him declaiming the Gettysburg Address in a very un-American accent."

And in Kyoto I was befriended by Mary McCrimmon, who taught at the university there. She invited me to the Japanese home where she lived for a traditional tea ceremony, to be followed by an informal family supper.

Although it was warm, her landlady had spent the whole morning making the sweetmeats that were demanded by the ceremony. When we arrived in the early afternoon, she was still in housedress and perspiration, her hair straggling. Mary briefed me while we waited in the comparative cool of the garden: no talking, hands to be held just so, each of us to kneel on a special cushion to accept the tea bowl, and remember to turn the bowl towards the hostess before taking the ceremonial sip.

"Poor Mrs. Tamaki looked hot and had been working all day in the kitchen. I felt miserable to be the occasion of it all. But once the tea ceremony began, I forgot everything but its beauty. Mrs. T appeared, lovely, serene, in a beautiful grey-blue kimono. Mr. T, composed, expressionless, resigned? to my right. Mary and I kneeling properly and anxious to see and observe the ritual. Mrs. T's movements with the jar of tea powder, her meticulous dusting of each utensil, her careful folding and refolding of the green silk cloth she used to wipe the bowl, her deftness with the tiny long-handled tea spoon – all these were a joy to watch, seriously done, with a sort of quiet dedication that was impressive. And the ritual quality of handing the tea to the first guest, the turning of the bowl to face the hostess, the apology to the next guest, the acceptance, all very formal. The cold tea itself, whisked to stir the powder into cold water, was bright green and delicious." In atmosphere it was so like an Anglican Eucharist that I felt quite at home.

And the garden supper afterwards was reminiscent of many family outdoor meals that I have shared with the Woods, different, but alike. The garden was small, defined by shrubs with leaves of different colours and contrasting textures. Mr. T and his tall son carried out a low table from the living-room. The daughters and Mary put four straw mats around it for us to kneel on. Every time you stepped off the mat on to the grass you wiggled your feet into clogs, and out of them again at the kitchen door. It was a great occasion for the Tamakis as well as for us because the new garden was being used for the first time, and Mr. T took pictures madly, just like Roy or Dawson.

Mary took me to Nara, an ancient holy city, and ensconced me there in the guest-house of a small Buddhist monastery. This was something like a youth hostel, a long row of small rooms, each open to the narrow deck that ran all along the outside wall. Each room had one low table, cushions to sit on, and its inner wall was a sliding cupboard holding the floor pad that could be spread out for the night. Paper panels slid across the open side to give one privacy. Mary and the other friends who came for the weekend went back to Kyoto, leaving me alone for the week with only sign language to share with the priest and his wife.

"The evening was one of the most piquant I have spent anywhere, with Mrs. Nakata [the diminutive wife of the priest in charge, and my hostess] entertaining me – desperately – but sweetly, singing a Japanese lullaby and other Japanese songs, then *Santa Lucia* and *Old Folks at Home* in Japanese. I sang to her *Vive la Canadienne, En Roulant Ma Boule Roulant*, the Iroquois Lullaby, and so on. Then she found a book of her husband's that had Japanese and English words and simple part arrangements, so we sang together. The little thing is so merry, and so earnest, and so direct. I loved her.

"But I was utterly rocked this morning when Mrs. N came purposefully out to keep me company on my walk. I was surprised and appalled at first, then terribly amused, and finally touched. We had a lovely walk together, understanding each other better than words might have let us, sharing the silence, the majesty of the great trees, the cool duskiness of the woods, while I took pictures, including one of her that she didn't know about."

I left Japan in love with the people and the gardens, but after the confusion and heat of Tokyo, Hong Kong seemed like heaven.

"What a lovely city – how lucid – how British – how clean and white and colourful after Japan's blacks and browns and ochres. I can read the road signs. There are Belisha beacons. Taxis don't aim at you. I actually saw a car slow down for a pedestrian. And for 20¢ HK one can cross on the ferry with a fresh breeze and beautiful Hong Kong in one direction and beautiful Kowloon in the other."

I was booked to join a tour to be taken to China for a few weeks. But at the last minute we were refused visas. It was a famine year in China, and the authorities didn't want tourists. I went ahead of schedule to New Zealand

for a month of painting and staying with friends. Ella
Forbes was the little Scottish woman who had been
quietly crying beside Ginny and me as the ship pulled
away from Glasgow in 1951, at the end of our Wonderful
Year. We were mopping up too, and our shared tears had
served as an introduction. She was the main reason I was
going to New Zealand, she and Margaret Wills, who had
taught with us in the art department at Central Tech for
a few months. While touring the world, Margaret had
found herself a job with the Toronto Board of Education
as a supply teacher. Once Charlie Goldhamer found out
what a good art teacher she was, he kept her busy full
time, as one after another of us was able at long last to go
home to bed when sick. Margaret lived in New Zealand's
North Island, and Ella in the South. I visited each of them,
and then brought them together for a holiday week in a
cottage on a lake near Rotorua, a change and a treat for
us all.

Looking back, I find it hard to know why my sketches
in Japan and New Zealand were so uninspired. I worked;
always I keep on painting through a dry period, hoping
that sometime the juices will start running again. Japan
was so exotic it should have given me great stimulus, but
my paintings were pedestrian, illustrations rather than
expressions. I destroyed all but four of the ones I made
there. However, by the end of my third week in Blenheim,
where Ella lived, things improved, and a little magic
began to creep in. I can remember sitting on a grassy
hillside above the village, saying out loud to myself, "Talk
about it. Don't try to imitate it. *Tell* it, don't *show* it."

So as to be able to carry everything myself, I had made
a light portfolio with handles to hold my paper and

drawing-board, and a knapsack for such essentials as
paints, water jar, blow-up cushion, and slicker, as well as
an easel-bag that went over my shoulder, all of fabric-
backed plastic. Two small, soft-top suitcases held everything else. Anything I bought or accumulated I shipped
home. By the end of my month in New Zealand I had
walked away my only pair of serviceable shoes. On my
last day there I bought a new pair and threw out the old
ones.

This was the second serious error of my trip, far worse
than the missing air ticket. I flew on to Singapore, back
into tropical heat, and in three days I had damaged my
poor feet irreparably. They swelled, and the shoes didn't.
At last I limped out of the hotel as far as a street vendor
and bought a pair of simple sandles with a thong between
the toes. Twenty-five cents, and release from torture. So
that, dear friends, is why from that time on I have gone
clip-clopping through life in "thongies." And why to this
day I can seldom find a dress shoe that doesn't hurt,
especially when the room is warm.

Singapore is where I first met the large ceiling fans that
make life bearable for foreigners in hot countries. Baths,
beer, and the ceiling fan was how I survived the tropics.
Many times that year I had flashes of insight into the
inwardness of Romeo's cry, "Banishment! . . . Do not say
banishment!" My world-travel project felt many times
like a fourteen-month sentence that I had to serve with
no time off for good behaviour.

In Thailand I stayed in a small hotel in Bangkok, lonely,
as I often was in strange hotels. I heard someone speak

English, and saw two young women, one obviously Thai, the other a Westerner. They were gracious when I approached them, and added a new chapter to the small-world cliché by having been nurses together in the New Zealand village of Blenheim, from which I had just come. They introduced me to a delicacy of the country, ice cream made from coconut milk, very good.

At the Bangkok palace of Anna's King of Siam there was a scale model of the temple complex of Angkor Wat, the great Khmer ruins of which I had not even heard until then. These ruins were discovered less than a century ago almost by accident when a French explorer was hacking his way through the jungle. He came across something too solid to chop through, and when he tried to go around, he found himself following along a masonry wall. Before he came to the end, he realized that he had stumbled across a great work of architecture.

The model convinced me that I must see the original, and I did, after an epic wrestle with red tape. Cambodia was even then unsettled, but any active war was farther east than Angkor Wat, and the ruins were still in good condition. By the time I had dealt with the difficulties of getting there, physical and official, I was tired out. To see and photograph the sculptures I lay on the stone floor, flat out, exhausted but happy. This was mistake number three. I caught a severe cold that dogged me for weeks.

In the Cambodian hotel there was an English girl, also on her own, who teamed up with me to hire a jeep for a journey through the jungle to another temple that was highly recommended. It was a chance I couldn't miss, even if I was feeling miserable.

"September 18: I gratefully left this inhospitable room,

with my voice falling to my boots, real congestion of the chest, my back aching, my tummy nervous, and a feeling that a jeep ride was apt to be broken by hasty retreats into the bushes for various purposes. When we were met by the guide who was supposed to be driving us out, he looked gloomy.

"'Il n'y a pas un jeep. Il n'y a qu'un deux chevaux.' *Two horses*? We were aghast. Twenty miles through the jungle on a horse, and I hadn't ridden since that summer in the Rockies twenty-eight years before. We were still wondering how to cancel the arrangement when the 'deux-chevaux' was driven up, proving to be a two-horsepower Citroen car."

India a few days later was too rich, too diverse, too crowded, and too difficult for me. My best week there was at Khajuraho, in central India, an ancient royal city of many temples. The air service to Khajuraho was not operating yet after the rainy season, so a by-product of my decision to go there was a trip overnight in a train, with the passengers ranged in open bunks along the sides, wriggling in and out of their clothing inside the privacy of a thin sheet. I was the only woman travelling that night. There was no food service that I was able to discover, and it had not occurred to me to take emergency rations. In mid-morning, hollow with hunger, I was debouched at a station beside a road down which the bus to the village of Khajuraho was due to come. Mercifully, someone turned up with a barrow of fruit, and I was able to buy an apple.

In Khajuraho I spent my days drawing and painting the erotic sculptures that covered every surface of the temples. I had done enough reading to have some understanding of Hinduism and the importance of the god

Shiva as the source of fertility and creativity. Human sexuality is the natural symbol of that aspect of the god. Those sculptures were gorgeous. The week was too short.

I returned to New Delhi to arrange the obligatory visit to the Taj Mahal at Agra. It had its moments, but I began to feel that I could take the pressure of people no longer. I flew north and gave myself a week in a houseboat up in Kashmir, surely the most exquisitely beautiful place on the face of the earth. I lived on the quiet backwater of a lake ringed with snow-capped mountains. There I had the solitude I was desperate for, broken by a constant traffic of birds, exotic and colourful. Theoretically I had a staff of five, but the only ones in evidence were a houseman and a small boy. That was plenty. The houseman drew my bath, prepared and served all my meals, but did not protect me from the hawkers who came up in their little boats to sell carpets, fabrics, copper pots, flowers, antiques, and jewellery. After all, I would be gone in a week, and these pedlars were his year-long neighbours.

This was Muslim country, and my houseman, Mohammed, warned me that on Friday morning he would be going to the mosque, too early to be able to bring me my usual wake-up tea. "Will you be making a fire for your own breakfast before you go?" I asked. "Then please bring me tea before you leave, whenever it is." And he did, about 3:30 A.M. The least I could do was to accept the tea with many thanks and offer him my good wishes for a pleasant walk to the mosque through the pre-dawn darkness.

From India I moved into Afghanistan, a refreshing change from the sticky heat, from the outstretched hand and the cringing poverty. In Kabul the hotel was no less

inefficient, but my room-boy looked me in the eye as to
an equal, and if he brought me an electric lightbulb to
replace the burnt-out one, it was with the air of doing me
a favour.

The best time in Afghanistan was an adventure into the
back country. Hurlimann's book on Asia had included a
photograph of a huge figure of Buddha carved out of the
clay cliff in the valley of Bamian. To go there required a
special government pass, a licensed guide, and a driver.
This put a sizable hole in my budget but turned out to be
worth the fuss and expense. We left the twentieth-cen-
tury world of plastic and paint, and drove through countryside that was clay and ochre stone; even the grasses
had dried to straw colour. The rare farm compounds
might have grown out of the earth. Except for a few army
trucks, traffic was by donkey or horse. Much of our road
climbed through hilly wasteland covered with broken
rocks, the very wilderness of the New Testament.

But the valley of Bamian lay green about its little river,
bordered by golden poplars. We set out on foot to explore
the colossal sculpture, up a twisting stairway cut inside
the cliff, lit by deep slits in the clay wall, and came out on
a broad convex plateau under a domed roof, from which
we could look over the whole valley and across to the
small white box that was our hotel. We were on the head
of the great Buddha, and there was no railing to keep us
there.

It was September, but the frost had already coloured
the trees. Although our chicken dinner was warm and
good, the hotel boasted no heat and was too cool for
sitting around. I retired early to my chilly little bedroom
on the second floor, whose bath was innocent of hot water.

I was cold, every bit of me, unable to summon enough body heat to warm up the bedding. After shivering for a while without effect, I rang for the room-boy and asked him for a hot-water bottle. Twenty minutes later he returned with my guide, who explained that nobody had ever heard of a hot-water bottle. I agreed to settle for any screw-topped bottle or a gasoline tin – anything at all that would hold some hot water. Twenty minutes more went by before he returned with a long-necked cut-glass carafe with a glass stopper, full of hot water. I slept that night with one arm encircling the carafe and whatever I could find, clothes, knapsack, a second pillow, buttressing it against any movement in my sleep.

On to Iran. "Persepolis, September 23: I went over to the remains of the palace yesterday morning and wandered about taking photographs, then settled by the gate to draw one of the big figures of a bull with a human head. A Persian guard threw me completely by sitting on the wall above me and watching every stroke. I gave up and found a place where I had my back against a plinth that he couldn't climb, and worked out an idea that I liked. And at the end of the afternoon, for the lovely hour between the sun and the moon, I sat against a rock and played the recorder, enjoying the thin sweet melody in that big romantic setting."

From Iran I planned to move on to Iraq, at that time a police state. Even at its embassy in Iran, where I had to waste time waiting around to secure a visa, one could feel the oppressive atmosphere.

"Tehran, October 18: Taxi back to the Iraqi embassy for the papers I needed. It was a comical demonstration of petty officialdom being petty and officious. He was a stout dead-pan, without humour or warmth, without even courtesy. And he sat at a desk doing sums laboriously and copying them on to another sheet of paper while the group grew around him. When he asked me for 152 rials, and of course I had no coins, an unseen hand from behind me passed over two rials, and the action turned the individuals standing around waiting for their passports to be stamped into a group with a common interest and some sense of solidarity. When the official left the room, we talked together with the same release from constraint as if the teacher were out."

I was going to Iraq because it had the ruins of Babylon that I wanted to record and because Baghdad had a museum full of sculptures from the very first Sumerian civilization. Someone I had met in Iran had given me the name of a modest hotel and a letter of personal introduction to the owner.

My first impression was not good. "Iraq, October 19: Michael had better be good to be worth the struggle. I am sitting gingerly on the veranda, stewing mildly in the heat left by the sinking sun, observing a thick layer of dust, cigarette and cigar butts, dead leaves, paper, etc., on the floor, recalling the swivelling eyes of the character who greeted me. I'm sure it's a physical deformity. It's too much of a caricature to be a mere mannerism. The tea is weak but not bad, the biscuits crisp but stale-tasting. I think I'm in the wrong place, but how to leave?"

The individual with the swivelling eyes brought me a message from the owner asking me to meet him in the bar after dinner. Michael turned out to be a stout Arab whom I judged to be a bit younger than I. He greeted me with great warmth and asked me to share a drink and get

acquainted. Apparently he trusted the friends who had
sent me to him, and he talked freely of the hazards of the
political climate. Iraq was being wooed by the Soviets at
that time, and there were several groups of Russians
staying in the hotel. He was very interested in me and my
travels. I cannot remember ever having been so admired,
so showered with flattering attentions. Even to have free
choice from a whole bar full of bottles was a novel
pleasure.

"October 19: George Adams, the American ambassador, dropped in, and then a little Yorkshireman who
seemed to live in the hotel. It was quite educational, and
now I'm on their side and involved in the decay of fortune
that I saw before. It's very Hardyish."

"October 21: This extraordinary dismal Baghdad,
which I disliked so heartily on sight, certainly is giving
me a stranger bag of riches than better places have.
Yesterday was a day. I went out early in the morning into
a Sabbath emptiness, it being Friday, and picked my way
gingerly around the puddles and suspicious-looking fragments, breathing shallowly for fear of smells, to the second bridge. Things were livelier down there, street
vendors, strollers, idlers, but they still didn't know where
the Iraqi museum was. It was an urchin who found it for
me. It's terrific to see in the alabaster those stiff, staring,
Sumerian votive figures, all the jewellery from Ur, and
pictures showing the tomb where they were found. My
old friends Dudu and Gudea, best of the ancient sculptures, were there in stone.

"And so we sat in the bar last night sipping liqueur,
discussing sandwiches and timetables for tomorrow,
while Michael flattered me with his words, with his 'May

I say this to you? You won't be cross with Michael? May I tell you what I would like?' and I realized that here was someone who had made of seduction a fine art form, bold and vigorous but also subtle and sensitive. My insatiable curiosity and my sheer sex hunger were working with him. I discovered myself becoming vulnerable to his charm and powerful sex appeal. Every principle and every bit of common sense told me that his courtship was outrageous, but every nerve in my body was responding with desire. Last night even I was charmed by my reflection in the bar mirror. I looked fair and gay and altogether delicious."

We were to drive out into the desert with our picnic and wine packed in a basket, there to explore the pleasures of love under the stars. I knew that if I stayed around I would yield, and I fled. I would be less than human if I had no regrets that I missed the experience he was offering. But I was protected by long habits of respectability and my genuine mirth at his pressing invitation to stay for a fortnight "as Michael's guest."

Thinking about it afterwards, I wrote, "I realized in one of my rumination periods yesterday that the artistic expression of love, if it cannot be hurried on the occasion, can be hurried even less in the situation. The thoughtfulness, heightened companionship, the development of rituals and private language are all part of loving even in its purely sexual sense. Being in love is necessary for sex, and then it can be an art. Nothing less is good enough. I'll be damned if I'll ever settle for less."

I escaped, advancing my flight to Lebanon in order to miss the Saturday-night date he was pleading for.

"It hurt me to leave without goodbye this morning. We

said it last night – he's no morning lark. The moral seems to be that there is no safe age for dalliance for anyone of my temperament. There is one consoling little detail. I was invited to lunch by Jacqueline, a friend of his, and when she gave me an opening, I asked her how she handled a date with Michael to keep him tame. 'Oh, he's not a bit like that,' she assured me cheerfully, and I gulped deeply and said I was glad to hear it and that I must have been imagining things. This I have cherished because it suggests that his reaction to me was personal, and not just because I was a woman."

Istanbul, which I reached early in November, became my third-favourite city in the world, trailing only London and Rome. There were some problems, particularly in obtaining permission to take photographs inside the great Byzantine church Saint Sophia. It is an enormous and glorious building, impossible to imagine from any photograph I have ever seen of it. When it was converted from a Christian church to a mosque, the authorities whitewashed all the mosaics and hung gigantic round panels with texts in Islamic script, hiding the bones of the building and spoiling its coherence. Although photography is strictly forbidden, I carried an introduction to the director, who agreed to let me photograph the interior, that afternoon only and without a tripod.

"It's *most* difficult. My average exposure was eight seconds, with no way of steadying the camera. A flash was hopeless in that huge place. But I kept slugging away until the dramatic moment when a zealous Turkish guide pulled my camera out of my hand, tripped the shutter, and

looked as if he would tear out the film. I returned fury for
fury and ordered him to follow me to the office, and as
we marched towards authority he began to suspect his
mistake and subside." He spoke only Turkish and I only
English, but as we raged at each other, we certainly
communicated. By the time the confrontation was over, I
was shaking so that any possibility of hand-holding a
camera was over for that day. My permit was extended
to the morrow, and when I finished the next morning I
was hopeful that I had at least a few pictures that would
capture some of the glory.

"Izmir, Turkey, November 13: Tonight I am *drunk* – on
one half-bottle of red wine and one archaeologist, a darling, Turkish, dark, serious, sweet, with almost enough
English. I understood everything he said. I don't know
how well he followed me, but by mutual agreement we
spent all day together, from the time I presented my
credentials in the morning, through lunch, when I happened into the same café. He welcomed me to his table
and then put his head down and ate in silence, to my
amusement, but came up at the grapes course and offered
me a sociable Turkish coffee at the end, brought from
elsewhere. I liked this man and was very attracted to him,
and grateful that he said or did nothing to tell me that he
was also attracted to me, although I knew it. What a very
decent man, small in worldly terms, still with his university degrees to finish, probably on a mean salary, Turkey
his horizon but in love with his work, writing poetry
about it. Wonder where he keeps his wife and children.
He has them, but it was a fly-blown restaurant at noon.
So what of the ruins of Ephesus? The museum? The
church of St. John? The double church of the Virgin? All

seen across a pair of brown eyes and a young but lined
face, a strong, fine face, in a clean white sport shirt with
a slightly shabby tweed suit. I'm glad I took some pictures
of him. Tomorrow I shall insist on a smile."

I was due to return the next day to take photographs
of the sculptures in the museum and the ruins of old
Ephesus, which lay a couple of miles away from the
village.

"November 14: No smile captured on film, but a couple
of memorable ones. Especially the one that greeted me as
he leapt off the tractor coming to meet me on my walk
from old Ephesus back to the village."

When I had arrived by bus from Izmir in the morning
and gone along to the Ephesus museum, I was given the
welcome reserved for friends of the director. God forbid
that anyone should take a ticket from *me*, etc. The very
decent little guard knew the exhibits and briefed me on
date and subject while I listed what I wanted to photograph. Then I trailed up the hill to the basilica, where the
archaeological work was in progress, leisurely, enjoying
and savouring the occasion. My director friend Musa
Baran was not in the office. A workman waved me to the
east, and I made a circuitous descent to get down to where
I could see him measuring with one end of a long tape.
Small girls chorused "Bye-bye" at me, and I arrived down
in a chant of bye-byes. We were brief and businesslike. I
told him my plans. He agreed and I left him to his work,
and sailed on down to the museum, hoping en route that
the staff would take my word for it that I had his permission. I needn't have worried. He was there while I was
still screwing on the flash attachment, and hovering about
while the guard and I did our stuff. By 12:30 I had

finished, and I went off to ancient Ephesus with a firm agreement to come to see him if he didn't get out there.

"And a glorious day I had at Ephesus. I felt the red carpet everywhere. The guards were helpful but respectful and left me alone. After lunch I clambered over fragments until I found a moulding shaped for me, and eased myself into it with my feet up on a fine stone base, and wrote to Flo, and purred and thanked God for the sweet sun, the sweet air, the sweet silence, the sweet archaeologist, then down for a comb-up and wash beside the little arbour restaurant, face, hands, feet, and tea that could teach the Izmir Palas a thing or two, ready for the walk into town. I overtook two or three natives en route, but my pace was too good for them, and we parted. Some women picking cotton hailed me, and enjoyed a good laugh over our shared greeting, and when I turned on to the long stretch, the tractor was coming, and there he was, grinning boyishly but tongue-tied, and we fell into step without apology or explanation, and it was a lovely evening, a lovely walk, an obvious fellowship. We detoured to see the recently excavated Artemis temple, one large blank to me but important and full of meaning to him. But of course we came to the bus stop at last, and the bus came rattling up and I was on it before I had time to realize it. He probably didn't understand half the nice things I said to him, but it was a pleasure to say them. And I hope he gets some fun out of the strong pattern of my sandals all over his Ephesian dust."

In Greece I followed the routine that had gradually become established, to fly into the capital city, explore the

cathedrals or temples and the major museums, then escape up-country to a smaller place to live and perhaps
paint for a week or so. Athens was even better than my
memories of it. The Acropolis welcomed me as a daughter, every aspect of it already known and loved, but still
leaving me in awe. I told Ginny when I wrote to her that,
like God, the Parthenon *is* and can only be worshipped.
It was when I came down with another heavy cold that it
began to dawn on me that it was hard, tiring work flying
into a new country, into an unknown language, where
even the signs were in a strange alphabet, and the cur-
rency unfamiliar. No wonder I was exhausted on first
arrival, and perhaps I should remember next time not to
collapse on to cold stone floors.

That cold was my excuse for the most luxurious and
spectacularly beautiful stopping-place of my year. At
Delphi, a hundred miles or so north of Athens, I settled
into a hotel with central heating, in a spacious room
overlooking the whole magnificent valley, with a big
private bathroom with hot and cold running that was as
good as its word. Expensive for a hotel but cheap for a
hospital was how I rationalized it.

Certainly Delphi was a place for healing, although
there were echoes of tragedy in it too. "After spending
time with the bronze charioteer in the museum, I drifted
on down to the sacred spring of Eleusis. Fourteen eagles
were circling above the great stone heights from which
blasphemers were cast. It was easy to picture them up
there on the edge, while the crowds waited below for the
ghastly and wonderful moment when the tiny figure
should hurtle out into the sky and toss from rock to rock
as it came smashing down to the ledges below. Were there

trumpets to warn the crowd that the moment had come?
And how long did it take for the sound to follow the sight?
How many executioners and officials took the laborious
trek up the back of the mountain? Was the victim alone,
or one of several? Did he walk? Or was he tied to a
donkey? It all seemed credible and horrifying as you
looked up at that towering sharp hanging peak."

I had to drag myself away from Greece, but I was
booked to fly to Egypt early in December. In Cairo I went
first to the big archaeological museum. Twenty-five years
later the Royal Ontario Museum in Toronto was able to
show a tiny sample of its treasures, and the line-ups
waiting to see them stretched for blocks. I had that enormous building, packed with riches, almost to myself, and
every opportunity to browse, to photograph, to revel. The
incredible array of gold artefacts from Tutankhamen's
tomb filled the whole length of one big gallery. Other
galleries held the astonishing succession of sarcophagi,
each richer than the last, that had protected his mummy.

A couple of days later I took a crowded rush-hour bus
out to Giza, where the great pyramids are, and found
myself a place to stay with a window that looked towards
the largest. The next morning I discovered that the *son et
lumière* program that evening was to be in English. After
exploring all day, I was happy to find a seat early, and
while I was putting in time reading and catching up in my
journal, I heard behind me a party of men arrive, deep in
talk that seemed to have social and political overtones. As
I listened, I wondered to hear a very English voice telling
the Egyptians about their own country. I wondered still
more at the respect with which his pronouncements were
received, until I heard someone address him as Mr.

Toynbee and realized that I was in the presence of the great historian Arnold Toynbee, whose overview of the world civilizations, *A Study of History*, was a landmark work of the decade.

It was dusk before the program began. The lights went out behind us. Our own shadows disappeared, the stars came up, and one of the pyramids began to glow gently. The thing was well done. Best was the emergence against the coolly lit pyramids of the golden head of the Sphinx, its cheek contours illuminated so skilfully that the features were restored to the face. We saw it clearly, its calm beauty, its Mona Lisa smile, and the sound and light took us from the Great Pyramid to the building of the second, to the third, through the history, our attention directed now this way, now that. As each pyramid was being built in our minds, the light picked out the stones, moving slowly upward so that we saw it growing, course by course until it stood complete in its powerful clarity and perfection. At the end, as the voices rose in a crescendo affirming that "the works of man crumble into dust but the spirit of man lives on," an eagle, circling above the head of the Sphinx, caught the light on his wings and rose higher and higher into the darkness of the sky. It seemed a dramatic symbol of the spirit living on; there was no way *that* could have been contrived.

"Luxor, December 8: I find I rather fancy myself as a cyclist. There's the old problem of bruised bones against the saddle, but my legs are standing up nobly to the test. I cycled up to Karnak this morning amid cries of 'Baksheesh! Baksheesh!' and by the time I had wandered around for two and a half hours, I was weary and came speeding home to beer."

A beautiful Swedish opera singer under orders to rest her voice, a French girl who worked in Geneva, and two charming Swiss lads joined me on bicycles, and we made a congenial group, becoming such good friends in three days that our last night at Luxor was a hilarious dinner-party at one of the back-street restaurants. "Wine and food soon had us all feeling very gay, and Kirstin Meyer entertained us with marvellous stories of her concert tours, the performance in Venice where they opened to an empty house and the audience who did gradually arrive, left while they were still singing, to catch the last vaporetta, the glamorous ride home by gondola in the froth of evening dresses. We laughed our way home through the silent streets."

The return to Cairo was darkened by the discovery that I had mistaken the roll of film I had shot in Istanbul for a new reel, and used it over again at Karnak. Thirty-six double exposures, all useless. Saint Sophia lost. So much for my taking new films out of their cardboard boxes to save space and weight. This was perhaps the worst moment of the year, and all my own fault.

My peregrinations back and forth across the Mediterranean were planned so that I could spend Christmas in the Holy Land. I was booked into a former monastery on the Mount of Scandals, across the valley from the old walled city. Jerusalem, its domes, towers, minarets, dominated by the great Dome of the Rock, lay like a beautiful tapestry on the far hillside. This was before the Seven Days' War had given Israel the city and high-rises were allowed to modernize its appearance.

It was late afternoon before I reached the hotel. Already the sky was apricot below the clouds. But I couldn't

wait until morning to set foot in Jerusalem. I could see
the road, down into the valley (into the Vale of Siloam,
magic words) and up the other side to the city gate, two
or three kilometres, no more. It was an easy walk, and the
city was enthralling. I had no particular objectives, just
the pleasure of the golden ochre stone of the buildings,
the archways beckoning, the narrow streets, made mysterious as it grew dark by shadows too deep to see into. I
had soon lost my sense of direction and was poring over
my map of the city under a street lamp, trying to locate
myself, when a young Arab noticed me.

"Can I help you?" in excellent English.

He looked all right, and I did need help. "Could you
show me how to get to Herod's Gate?" "Come with me."
I let him lead me along streets that were strange to me,
through alleys so narrow that I wondered if they could
possibly be the right way. He was interested that I was a
Canadian, and especially that I was an artist and teacher.
He wanted to study art himself, but he had a job and there
was no night school. What was his job? He worked for
an electricity company, reading meters at Bethany. I can
still hardly reconcile the idea of Bethany, where Lazarus
was raised from the dead, with an electric meter.

At Herod's Gate, Shukri diffidently invited me to be
his guest for a sweet in the little café outside the gate. We
talked for another hour, and he walked me home to the
hotel, promising to call for me the following evening and
take me to explore Bethany. After the Bethany evening I
was a guest in his home for dinner and met all his family.
Shukri is still my friend, now settled in Michigan with an
art business of his own. He and his American wife come
to Toronto occasionally, most recently to share in the

celebration of the launching of the first part of this autobiography.

Dino was living in Rome, no longer a student on a meagre
fellowship but a mature artist working for the Food and
Agriculture Organization of the United Nations. We had
been in correspondence, and I was invited, for my first
weekend in Italy, to stay in his house. By Roman standards it was commodious, a two-storey flat with two big
bedrooms upstairs, and downstairs one wall all window,
which let in the sun and lit the whole depth of the main
floor. The Christmas tree and all the decorations were still
in place when I arrived, and my first meal there is a hazy
memory of candlelight, red wine, and laughter with Dino
and his closest friends, Zev and Gertrude.

Zev was an artist, an expatriate American whose work
was imaginative, irreverent, with some of the fey quality
I associate with Marc Chagall. He and Gertrude lived a
few blocks away from Dino, also in the centre of the city.
Dino was in love with all of Italy, and especially Rome.
His recreation was drawing its buildings, its people, its
life, in free linear style, whimsical, evocative rather than
literal.

I had arranged to buy myself a small Fiat car now that
I was on the comparatively solid (and familiar) ground of
Europe. It would give me a mobile studio and a way of
travel for the rest of the year. It would be ready for me to
pick up in a few days. I cannot quite remember by what
small steps I became an accepted member of the company,
but before long I was settled at Via Modena, with a routine
of seeing Dino off to work in the morning, having my own

breakfast and washing up, then taking off in my car, usually down to the Forum, where I could work hour after hour in blessed peace. By the time the light was failing in the afternoon, I was ready for home. It was my pleasure to do the shopping, gradually learning the Italian names for what we needed, and delighted by the friend-liness of the local shopkeepers. I had dinner ready for Dino when he came home after work. I think it was in the second week that he asked me as tactfully as he could whether we hadn't had enough potatoes and carrots for the duration. I saw the point and began to look for alternatives.

Dino took a mischievous delight in taking me around to the parties as "mia professore" and seeing the suspicion in the eyes of the young women, who, conscious of his eligibility, had been nursing hopes. I didn't blame them. I only wished their suspicions had been justified. But even without any element of romance in those months, I was living in heaven. We both had a rich awareness of the comedy of every day, and we laughed together from morning to night. Weekends were usually for exploring Rome and its environs, but sometimes on a Saturday Dino would gather the laundry that had been piling up in the big hamper and call for Zev, who would join us with his own load. We would drive in Dino's Volkswagen bug across Rome to the laundromat beyond St. Peter's. The boys had a routine. While the first load was being washed, we would repair to the bar next door, and by the time our coffee with grappa was finished, so was the washing. It dried during our second drink. Their technique of stretching and folding the sheets, and their merriment in

the process, reached the level of an art form. Then back
to Zev's, with time for me to pore over his recent paintings
while Gertrude was organizing the big feast of spaghetti
that was the climax of the day. I recall having my elbow
slip off the table as I tried in vain to keep my head propped
up and my eyes open through all the good talk that went
with generous goblets of wine.

Dino was enthralled with my slides, especially of
Greece, and realized that with me in residence he could
leave for a few weeks and see it for himself. He was due
for some holidays. I wanted him to go, but I was a bit
miffed that he was willing to leave me, and the thought
of being bereft of all that fun and fellowship was daunting.

"Rome, February 15: I may just as well get this out of
my system. Here I sit on the steps of the temple of
Antoninus and Faustina, with a winter wind blowing my
big board and my papers, and a winter sun keeping me
warm enough, *stewing*! I have just realized that if Dino
goes next week and stays a month, that is to all intents
and purposes the end of my time in Rome. There is
undoubtedly some injured vanity in here somewhere,
perhaps a lot of it, but also there is the memory of that
ghastly summer at Barachois when I tried to work and
live in isolation."

Then I was visited by inspiration. I might have Marjorie join me for a few weeks. I threw my paints and brushes
into their bag, gathered up easel and water jar, and made
for home, to spend an exciting hour talking to travel
agents and trying to work out dates and details, then
writing to Marjorie to see if it would be possible from her
end, and enclosing a cheque that would cover her air fare.

Dino made his noon phone call later than usual. "What was going on?" he complained. "The line was busy all the time. Did you leave the phone off the hook?"

"I have my own social life to look after," I returned airily, and with some satisfaction.

Roy, at some sacrifice, agreed to do without his wife for a while. Letters and cables flew across the Atlantic. And a few days after I had driven Dino to the station and seen him off, I was on my way down the highway bound for the Rome airport to meet my darling Marjorie.

It was twenty-six years, her whole married life, since we had had more than a single night together. Marjorie was a housewife and mother by conviction and vocation. I recognized and respected that. While she had been bringing up a lovely family and keeping Roy happy and fed, I had been all over the globe pursuing a hectic professional career, going through the one deep and serious attachment of my life, seven years of emotional turmoil through which she had followed me with her love and understanding. Her door was always open to me, her shoulder ready. And now, at last, I could offer her a couple of weeks of my world of travel. And we could be together day and night for a full fortnight, in beautiful and beloved Italy. No wonder I was excited.

Once I realized that the plane must have landed, I discovered that I was crying, and I still couldn't see her coming through the doors – no sign at the customs benches – and suddenly there she was, coming from a different direction, with a good-looking man in tow laden with all her bags and his.

I was so keyed up that I talked non-stop all the way to Rome, searching where to go to drop Marjorie's new acquaintance at his hotel, asking directions in Italian and understanding the answers, showing off shamelessly. Marjorie and I had no trouble persuading her friend that opera was more our speed than a night-club, and the three of us had a memorable evening together with *La Bohème*.

After a week in Rome, almost too social, thanks to Dino's friends rallying and our obligation to give return parties, we took off in my little Fiat for some of the places Marjorie wanted to see. I cherish a memory of Pompeii. We had spent the morning in the ruins and were at lunch at a small table outside a modest trattoria, deep in talk as usual. The waiter brought us a flagon of red wine, and Marjorie, still talking, pushed towards me for filling, not the juice glass but the tumbler beside it. I felt she had arrived.

From one chilly little hotel on the famous Amalfi Drive we brought back a phrase that served us all too well as the days went on. It was raining again, steadily. Italian hotels are seldom heated, and we were at breakfast in sweaters and jackets, exchanging greetings with a gentleman who spoke excellent English and remarked that the weather was indeed "very variable."

It kept on being very variable for almost the whole of our precious two weeks. I was longing to introduce Marjorie to my beloved Forum, but not in the rain, and it was our second-to-last day before we could risk it. I have a memory of her there on the Palatine Hill, in her black hat and purple sweater and skirt, her skin warm against the sky, her smile complete, with the sunlit towers and roofs of Rome below her.

Both of us were incredulous that it had actually happened. Since our childhood summers at Silver Island, almost forty years earlier, we had not lived together, and now as we drove down the highway to the airport, we could look back on fourteen days of full-time sharing. When she had gone on board and I was stranded in the spectators' balcony, I watched, through binoculars that were her parting gift to me, while the aircraft doors were shut, the front steps wheeled away, and the plane turned towards the runway. Quite suddenly I was desolate and fled, unable to watch the take-off.

Dino's return was a merry reunion that supported me through the ordeal of making plans to leave. We still had time for hearing about his month in Greece and for some good sightseeing together. My new binoculars brought the mosaics close enough to allow me to appreciate the subtleties and the details. I was annoyed that I had been without them for such a major part of my travels, a stupid decision to save weight and bulk.

A follow-up to the months in Rome was the satisfying evening at Fool's Paradise a year or two later, when at long last I had Marjorie and Dino under the same roof, with Roy and Dino's bride and Flo and Ginny to round out the party. Marjorie and Dino each said to me privately during the evening, "Why didn't you tell me what a marvellous person he/she was?" There had been no use trying to tell them, because no description of mine could capture either of them.

Travelling by myself in Spain was predictably lonely after Rome, but offered some consolations. I knew that Altamira was where the prehistoric cave paintings were, the charging bison so familiar in the history of art textbooks, but I couldn't find it on the map. At last I found someone in a tourist bureau who both spoke English and knew the answer. Apparently Altamira was the name of the cave, and to find it I had to get to Santander, a village up in the northeast corner of the country. As I drove north, the warm weather and the tender green of early spring changed to lowering skies with a raw wind. It was a long, weary drive, and by the time I reached Santander a wet snow was splattering the windshield and the road was treacherous with slush. Santander's only inn stood at the top of a hill from which the village straggled down a narrow street to the church square at the bottom. Inn and village seemed deserted. But the handbell that stood on the desk brought a young woman to look after me. She spoke no English, but her high-school French matched mine, and we were able to understand each other.

"No, Madame, the caves are not open today, but tomorrow they will be open after ten o'clock, and it would be possible to view them."

Did she have a "chambre pour moi pour deux nuits?"

"Mais oui, Madame," and dinner would be ready "à sept heures."

Half-way through the soup course I heard a rhythmic chant, distant but coming closer. Leaning out of the open dining-room window, I could see a procession coming up the hill from the church, singing, and stopping now and again while the leader intoned a prayer. Each time they resumed the singing, they surged ahead, climbing the village hill towards the inn. Behind them came six men in black robes with a litter on which lay a life-size wooden figure of Christ, naked except for a loincloth, the hands and feet limp and blood-stained.

"Where are they going?" I asked the young waiter who

was leaning out the window beside me. I recognized the word "cemetery" in his reply, and realized for the first time that this was Good Friday. I had been watching the re-enactment of the Entombment.

On Saturday I made my pilgrimage to the prehistoric cave paintings, satisfied to have seen the originals and hoping that my photographs would make better slides than I had been using. Then I wondered if the village church might offer some architectural interest, so after lunch I went down to explore. It was a desolate sight. All the doors gaped open. The altar was stripped bare. Behind it a black cloth hung from ceiling to floor. Benches were overturned, lying every which way in the aisles. Where one looked for statues, one saw heavy black shrouds. Even the doors leading from the church to the cloister and garden were hanging half open. God was dead and his house deserted.

I wandered disconsolately around, too depressed for photography. But a written notice on the door said something about sabado, 23 horas – eleven o'clock tonight? What then?

At a quarter to eleven I trailed down the hill again after a straggle of villagers bound for the church. This time the door was closed, and the crowd gathered in silence on the church steps. Promptly at eleven the priest came out, black garbed, and in the same strong voice I had heard before, spoke to us. I recognized the word "significación" and realized that he was explaining the ceremonies that were to come.

As we filed into the dark church, each of us was handed a candle. The priest, whose candle was the only one

lighted, led us up the side aisle to the back of the nave and
grouped us around the stone font there. With prayers and
the sprinkling of holy water he reconsecrated the baptis-
mal font and lit the candles on either side of it. We were
led back down the centre aisle and into the pews, which
had been replaced in rows in front of the sad, empty altar.
Again with prayers and holy water he sanctified the altar,
then dressed it in white linen, setting its cross in the centre
and lighting candles at both ends.

A service began that seemed to be familiar to the
congregation. They sang a hymn as if they knew it by
heart, and joined in responsive prayers. A taper lighted
from a candle on the altar was used to light the candle at
the end of each row. The light was passed along the row
until every candle was flaming, and the church began to
glow with light and warmth. More prayers and hymns
completed that part of the service, the candles were
extinguished, the priest retired into the vestry, and the
congregation knelt in silence.

When the priest returned he was resplendent in a white
brocade robe lavish with gold, and attended by two boys
in white linen tunics with deep borders of lace. The organ
played quietly. The priest began the liturgy of the mass,
still in the familiar Latin. I recognized bits, the readings
of the epistle and gospel, the credo. The service moved
on gradually towards the consecration of the bread and
wine. And then it happened.

As the priest pronounced the words, the acolytes rang
their little silver bells, the organ burst into majestic music,
all the lights in the church blazed into sudden brilliance,
and the black curtain behind the altar fell to the floor,

revealing a golden dazzle of saints and cherubim. In my mind, in my emotions, and in my senses, I experienced the miracle of the Resurrection.

Sunday afternoon I moved on into France, where two surprises lay in wait for me. The pleasant one was when I went into a strange church in a strange village just over the border from Spain and found myself surrounded by old friends. Ceiling and walls were covered in Romanesque frescoes that I had taught for years without ever knowing where the originals were located.

The less agreeable surprise was to discover the morning after arriving in Paris that my car had been broken into and robbed. My diary was still there, and, thank God, so were my bundle of paintings and the carton of slides. But the door had been forced, and camera and suitcases had vanished. I have wondered since how I could have borne it if the thieves had taken my year's work.

England was home-coming, and a solid six weeks of painting before it was time to welcome Flo and Ginny, who were to join me for the summer. To avoid having to pay duty on my new camera equipment, I had arranged to buy it in Canada and have Flo bring it to me. We shared a horrified moment when I opened the lens-case she had carried slung over her shoulder and found it empty. Apparently all the thieves were not French.

If my year of travelling with Virginia stays in my mind as the Wonderful Year, this trip by myself around the world is the Long Year. I don't regret any part of it. The thousands of slides of sculpture and architecture that I carried home made it possible for me to give students a vivid experience of the art of the distant past and share with them my enthusiasm for it. One of my satisfactions in the next ten years was receiving postcards from students, off by themselves in Europe or Asia, who were full of gratitude for having been introduced to the masterpieces they were now meeting in person. They were travelling with eyes trained to see.

The hardest discipline for me was to go on painting, slugging it out, without the encouragement and stimulus of someone to react to my work. For that I had to wait until the sketches were unpacked, sorted, finished or revised, and ready for exhibition.

It was good to have dipped into so many different and unfamiliar cultures and to have discovered for myself that when you have a chance to meet people and be with them, however briefly, there are no longer any strangers. Everywhere I had found kindness and goodwill. Even lack of a common language could not prevent some expression of friendliness.

One aspect of the year that surprised and pleased me was eye-contact with people I met on the street, in buses, anywhere. Was it because I looked at them first? At home I feel invisible unless the passer-by turns out to be an acquaintance who knows something about me. Then I am automatically thought of in my setting, my family, my work, my home or neighbourhood, but seldom known for myself. Abroad, especially in the Middle East, which I had most feared, I was seen by every passer-by, observed, and observed with interest and approval. With no context to define me, people saw *me*, and judged me by what they saw. I felt alive in myself, and not just in relation to society. I felt real.

4

Loss and Gain

COMING HOME TO Fool's Paradise was coming home to open arms, to my house in order, the garden tended, and the cats spoiled, all thanks to Ginty and Milly. It was as I had dreamed it when I dared let myself think of it at all. It was coming home to Marjorie, to Nan, to Malcolm, to the new studio, to Nicky and Josephine the kitten with the coat of many colours, and also to the September ordeal of starting a new school term with no momentum until I had created it.

"Saturday, October 26, 1962: The end of Daylight Saving, the night with the gift of an hour, practically my first free hour since I have returned, but an excuse to take time to write. Josey is missing, but I assume that she is out hunting. Nick is a black bundle in the excelsior at the bottom of one of the crates. The studio is a mess. The small table is deep in slides and empty slide magazines, crying to be sorted – oh delicious task. The big trestle table is

cleared for a session of mat cutting tomorrow. Cartons
and more cartons are piled around the stove, all the junk
cleared out of the garage today ready for burning. Picture
frames waiting to be filled and the tools to do it with are
in piles and stacks all over the room. It's cozy."

The next breathing space was after classes had ended
for the year. "Sunday, June 16, 1963: Today has been too
good to let pass. I woke to sunshine for my early coffee
hour, Nick warm and round on my left flank, a thrasher
sounding different enough on the big elm at the front to
get me out of bed for a look – the usual crowd of grackles,
starlings, redwings and a cowbird, with some low comedy
this morning when a feeble-minded baby starling landed
on the back of a grackle in the feeder."

If home was even better than my homesick thoughts
of it, Central Technical School was promising dramatic
improvements to the art department. Even before I had
left on my sabbatical, a new art building had been sketch-
ily planned, actually on the back of an envelope, drawn
in haste by Dawson while he and Charles were in a
meeting of the heads of departments. Many draft plans
later, with Macy DuBois the architect listening to our
needs and trying to meet them, ground was broken and
the building became visible. Second thoughts about the
budget had eliminated the plant-room that Dawson had
wanted so badly for the study of natural forms, and my
storage cupboard had been reduced to a frustrating four
feet wide by about thirty deep. But we were to be off by
ourselves in our own building with skylights and windows across the whole north side. From my classroom
there was a view of houses with backyards and trees,
riches.

We packed our equipment, books, and archives into
cartons before the Easter break, ready for the professional movers, and came back after the week at
Haliburton to our new home. But where were my precious still-life stands with the storage lockers underneath
them? I went pelting down to the office to inquire, and
from there to the telephone to chase Harvey Self, the
Board of Education boss of the physical aspects of the
system. I couldn't believe my ears when he told me that
they had been scrapped. It had taken me twenty-five
years to get exactly what I wanted and needed and they
had been thrown out? I demanded that they be restored,
but they had been sent to the dump, beyond recall, and I
never saw them again. And Harvey Self had the bad
judgement to suggest that he wanted the new room to
"look nice" and had eliminated my old cupboards on
aesthetic grounds. At that point I lost my temper and
informed him with bitterness and passion that nobody
cared as much about the appearance of my room as I, or
knew better what "looked nice." Two years later, at shock-
ing additional expense, some substitutes arrived, nothing
like so satisfactory. Instead of softwood backs that accepted thumbtacks gracefully, the new stands were of
heavy, resistant plywood, and I never liked them.

Interesting that there is always a price to be paid for
what you gain. The light-filled rooms were impossible for
teaching history of art with slides, and I had to build a
cupboard on wheels to hold my projector, reference
books, and the slides for the week, which I could trundle
along to the elevator and down to the basement level to a
free classroom with black-out curtains. Someone else
would be using my room while I was out of it, and I never

again had the security of being in full control of the situation there. Because we were now on three levels, it was no longer possible to step into the corridor and whisper "pssst" to summon the six senior teachers for an informal conference or to share a joke. Each classroom had its own sink, so no more meetings at the "village well." On the plus side, Charles put in a fine sound system and bought tapes of superb classical music. Bach and Vivaldi and Mozart welcomed us at the front door and coloured our day. And for the first time it became permissible for the girls and even the teachers to wear slacks in our own territory. (For a few years still it was compulsory to change into skirts to appear in the parent building for assembly or academic classes.)

Audrey Garwood, a fine young artist and a vital teacher, newly widowed with four small children, joined the staff. She bought a big house within walking distance of Tech. One day her little dachshund Maxie got loose, followed her, and came in to the school looking for her. Charles cared about dogs and was afraid that Maxie would be run over if he did that again. Audrey should bring him with her. From then on Maxie was understood by staff and students to be an honorary member of the art department. Audrey was small, stocky, with hair usually wild and often wildly coloured, who dressed dramatically and unconventionally. We enjoyed seeing them arrive, Audrey's sturdy gait echoed by her stocky little Max. At noon he joined us all in the staff common room, greeting each of us as we arrived and subsiding again under Audrey's chair. One day the vice-principal, who was responsible for discipline in the whole school, a good guy whom we liked and trusted, met Maxie in the front hall.

"What's that dog doing here?" he asked Charlie. "What dog?" Charles replied, looking him straight in the eye. Owen got the message and said no more.

The Toronto art scene was livelier than when I had gone off on my sabbatical. Catalogues of the juried exhibitions of the sixties show an eclectic mixture of styles and points of view, with abstraction and abstract expressionism increasingly dominating the galleries. Montreal and New York seemed to be providing much of the inspiration. Jack Bush, who had been very much a middle-of-the-road artist in my first years in the Ontario Society of Artists, was now producing large colour-field canvases, to critical acclaim.

I was given the senior painting classes, and I felt that after the sound grounding the students had received in the fundamentals, I should encourage them to experiment with modern developments. I began to give assignments that would make them explore some currently fashionable ways of working. One of the tasks I set was to create a painting using only two flat colours. The finished work must be satisfying and able to hold the viewer's interest, an aesthetic challenge. Another was to produce a good piece of "found art," for which the student was free to gather his material anywhere, animal, vegetable, or mineral, but must assemble or mount it so that it had the unity, the dynamism, the excitement, of any valid work of art. I showed the class a film of Karel Appel, the Dutch abstract-expressionist master, in which he filled a spatula with heavy paint and ran the length of his studio to gain momentum for the slashing stroke he made with it on the canvas. We moved outside to the playing-field south of the art building to free us from concern for the floor and walls. There the students flung paint around by the big brushful and let the drips run where they would. There were interesting studio sessions afterwards, when we judged the works and the students began to appreciate that the difference between good, bad, and indifferent was valid whatever the style or technique used. Because I wanted them to learn to evaluate their own work, my criticisms were usually Socratic. I asked them to look with me at this or that aspect, the composition, the balance of tone and colour, perspective if it was relevant, and make a critique. Often we spread out the work of the whole class and sat, pretending to be the jury for an exhibition, discussing the virtues and weaknesses of each. This was the practice that had been so helpful to me and my fellow artists on our painting trips to the Gaspé and Haliburton.

When I went with a class to the AGO to see a current exhibition, the students were as confident in judging the non-objective work as the representational. Their enthusiasm for a painting was sometimes a hint to me that I should take a more appreciative look. To develop my own discrimination I myself began to work in flat colour with hard edges, to eliminate detail and tell my story in the simplest form possible. I found this challenging and exciting.

Every spring during the sixties and for some time afterwards, Ginty and Milly moved in to Fool's Paradise as soon as they came up from Florida, and stayed with me until it was time for them to drive south for the winter. Ginty spoiled me, prepared all the meals, looked after the mail, adored the animals, and even kept the garden weeded. I began to appreciate what it must mean to a man to have a good wife.

Just after they had left for Florida in 1963, I was shocked
by a telephone call from my dear Madeline in California.
Frances, her seventeen-year-old daughter, my god-
daughter, was pregnant. Could I give her sanctuary, a
home to live in until the baby was born and ready for
adoption? This was an era when unmarried pregnancy
was still considered to be a disgrace and a major disaster.
Abortion was illegal and dangerous. Neither Frannie nor
her boy-friend was ready for marriage or the responsibility of caring for a child. Banishment during pregnancy
and giving up the baby for adoption was the discreet way
of handling the situation recommended by the social
agencies, and Toronto was far enough from San Francisco to forestall gossip at home. I hope my "Of course"
sounded more enthusiastic than I felt.

I was glad Madeline had turned to me for help, but the
prospect of having a teenager in the house full time was
somewhat daunting. Frannie had been an exquisite baby
but had grown into a wilful and destructive four- and
five-year-old, a menace on her visits to Fool's Paradise as
a child. The family moved to Quebec, and Madeline and
I had written often, but Frannie's school years were
passed out of my ken. I had seen very little of her in Palo
Alto on my way to Japan. Like most fifteen-year-olds she
had been detached from the family, busy with her teenaged friends. I just didn't know her.

She arrived a week later. I can see her still, her thick
auburn hair flying, chewing gum as she came through the
gate at the Toronto air terminal. My heart sank. The drive
home was as cordial as I knew how to make it, but we did
not seem to be making contact. And I thought that our
first meal would never end. Fran dawdled and dawdled

over her food. I have an obsession about time, and I could feel my impatience mounting. Finally I left her to it and got on with the evening chores.

I think Frannie and I both had a hard time for a few weeks in spite of our best efforts. I gave her the bed in my studio, where she would have the television, and cleared some storage space for her. She was not planning to do anything but rest up and get ready to have the baby. I soon lost my illusions that I would have a tidy house to come home to at the end of a school day, with the shopping done and some steps taken towards dinner. This was not going to be at all like having a good wife. More than once she was still in a dressing-gown, curled up on her bed with a magazine or enjoying a prolonged telephone call with a teenaged friend from her past. I marvelled that she could be content to be so idle.

Frances Dalziel, her other godmother and the one for whom she was named, would invite her for dinner sometimes, a break for us both. "Big Fran's" husband was an obstetrician, Frannie's doctor, and with five children at home their house must have been a welcome change from my spinster's retreat. Frannie had her driver's licence. I learned to respect her driving and trust her with my car. Remembering my own mother's mistakes, I also learned to go to bed and even to sleep while she was still out.

Early on, I asked her what she wanted me to tell people, and to my relief she said, "The truth." Once I had stopped expecting a young version of Ginty and was able to accept her the way she was, we became friends. She was a delightful companion, playful, and capable when she was interested. She loved festivities and undertook a major part in getting ready for the Christmas party that

year, baking, decorating, turning the chores into games.
By this time she was bulging unmistakably. Some of the
guests had known her as a child and were aware of the
situation, but when I introduced her to Bora Laskin, he
innocently asked her where her husband was. "I don't
have any husband," Frannie said cheerfully, and Bora,
after a noticeable gulp, went on to other topics. It was
Bora, dear kind Bora, who had a teenaged daughter
himself, who visited her in hospital and took her flowers
after the baby was born.

The birth was in January, on a teaching day. Frannie
woke me early with the alert, and Marjorie followed us
up to the hospital to stay with her while I went on to
school. She understood more than I could have what
Frannie was facing and was a far better surrogate mother.
That day cemented a strong bond between them. I was
permitted just once to see the baby, an exquisite little girl,
pink and white, incredibly like Frannie herself as a new
infant. The baby's father had visited us before Christmas,
full of reasonable arguments about why it was best for
the mother never to see her child. Frannie scorned the
advice. She chose to experience motherhood even for the
brief week she was allowed to keep the baby and nurse
her, and was willing to pay the inevitable price. It was hell
for all of us to give up that infant. She remained a pain in
our hearts from that day. There was to be a happy second
chapter to her story, but all in good time.

I was by this time vice-president of the Ontario Society
of Artists, ready for election to the presidency at the
annual meeting in the spring. I was succeeding Mac

Houstoun, who had succeeded Alan Collier, and I was
the first woman to be so honoured. I look back with some
irony to the exalted height this represented. The OSA was
the senior society of professional artists in Canada, still
housed in the Art Gallery of Ontario for its annual juried
shows. The formal openings of these exhibitions drew the
largest crowds of the year, more than two thousand. To
be elected president was a prestigious and heavy responsibility. I began months ahead to plan the big canvas that
I would submit to the jury for the annual exhibition. The
president's painting was traditionally hung in a conspicuous position in the long gallery, a dominant feature, and
I was determined that mine would be worthy.

It was worthy, but the campaign to oust the professional societies from the gallery was gaining momentum.
For ninety-odd years the society had elected a jury of
members, who had chosen the show from the hundreds
of works submitted, then arranged the accepted paintings
and sculpture to advantage in the rooms of the art gallery.
In 1964, my first year as president, the powers-that-were
at the AGO changed the rules. The society was no longer
privileged to hang its own show, and the gallery curator,
or whoever did the actual hanging, put my large vertical
canvas in one of the minor rooms and in a corner. Sic
transit gloria.

This was one more step in the gradual process by which
the art gallery manoeuvred the artists out. I cannot know
the politics of the campaign in detail. Fred Haines, a
painter and one of us, had been the director of the gallery
in the twenties. We were at home in the gallery then. He
was succeeded by Martin Baldwin, an architect and a
member of *the* Baldwins, one of Toronto's oldest families.

Secure in his connections and professional status, Martin made the decisions and worked well enough with the art societies. When he retired, the board appointed a young art teacher not long out of university to be the new director. It was widely assumed that the board or the women's committee, which was possibly the power behind the throne, wanted someone who would do its bidding, and that William Withrow was a man to be led, pushed, or persuaded to get rid of the art societies as regular exhibitors in the gallery. The powers-that-were coveted for the gallery an international profile and were enamoured of the New York avant-garde. When Withrow himself reached retirement, he described the Toronto art scene of that day as parochial, so he was in rapport with his masters.

The following year the Royal Canadian Academy and the OSA lost their traditional annual exhibitions. In 1965 both were absorbed into a joint open show organized and juried by the gallery.

The Art Institute of Ontario, represented by Paul Bennett, was doing a signal job of taking art to small communities and teaching them to see with new eyes. By 1960 Paul was organizing the circulation of thirty-two travelling exhibitions, sometimes taking them in his own van to the host town or village, meeting the local people and giving lectures to help them understand and appreciate the work. Five of the exhibitions that year had been created by the Ontario Society of Artists as special sections in their annual open show. By 1967 the number of exhibitions in circulation had more than doubled, and art films had been added. Many of the exhibitions had been newly created by the OSA, although some of the older ones were in such constant demand that they were kept in circulation for years. One of these wore out three sets of frames and was still being invited back. Paul and the society enjoyed mutual respect and worked closely together. We felt it as a personal blow when the Art Gallery of Ontario absorbed the Art Institute into its extension program and we lost Paul as an ambassador of visual art.

I can never thank Charles Goldhamer enough for his tolerance of the hours I spent on the work of the society. By the time I became president, my classes were almost all seniors, capable of working on their own. Those young artists knew that I cared about them and was ready to give generously whenever they came to me for criticism. But until they were in need of help, they left me at my desk in a welter of letters, notes, and telephone memos. They, and Charlie, accepted the hours and hours that I spent on the telephone engaged in the administration of the society.

The Ontario Society of Artists had operated for many years on a three-thousand-dollar annual grant from the Ontario Department of Education. With that we had been able to mount the annual exhibition, print an illustrated catalogue (which is today a valuable history of Canadian art), send educational shows travelling across the province, and pay for postage. I think we even gave a pittance to the secretary, who had a commercial-art business with an office and a typist who helped us out.

In my first year as president the Ontario Arts Council was set up, and swept away our grant with its new broom. From then on my life was an eighteen-hour-a-day struggle to keep the society's fiscal head above water. Our difficulties were compounded by the earlier conservatism of some of the members, who had been suspicious of the innovative and iconoclastic work of a few young artists and had voted down their applications for membership. Some of these rejected artists and OSA members Tom Hodgson, Oscar Cahén, Jack Bush, Harold Town, Alexandra Luke, Kazuo Nakamura, and Walter Yarwood formed Painters Eleven, which made a name for itself as the new avant-garde.

Because membership was by election, the OSA was sometimes accused of cliquishness and of allowing personal considerations to influence jury decisions. We bent over backwards to avoid this. A new jury was elected by ballot each year to make sure that there was a constant change of personnel. Cleeve Horne invented a remote-control voting device that prevented any jury member from knowing how the others had voted. I have a comic memory of that. The routine of jurying was for the chairman to wait until each work was placed at eye level in front of the jury and then ask, "Ready? – In? – Out? – Doubtful?" Each juror pressed a button hidden in his hand to record his vote, and the chairman counted the lights that appeared up on the board behind us after each category. The secretary noted the result, and the painting was removed and put into the appropriate pile. Once, when Peter Haworth was president and Cleeve Horne, York Wilson, and I were on the jury, one of the men saw a particularly hopeless painting being carried in. While Peter was momentarily distracted, he whispered that we should all vote it in. With deadpan faces we watched Peter's face as he saw all the lights go on after his question "In?" Peter took another look at the painting and tried the question again. Same result, and he was still sitting with his mouth open when we began to laugh.

When I became president, remembering my early experience of being refused membership (because I was too young and a woman), I succeeded in having the point system accepted, which allowed an artist, however unknown to us personally, to earn membership by having his work passed by three juries within a specified time-span.

In my second year as president we enlisted the help of a professional public-relations counsellor, Ed Parker, a terrific person. He interpreted public relations not as favourable publicity but as a program of community involvement, where we would contribute so much to the art scene that we would be sought out and used. Once a week I trailed down to Ed's office after school, tired after a full day of classes and the telephone, and allowed him to energize my imagination, so that I would drive home with a long list of new things that I could and should be doing to bring art into the lives of more people through the society.

We started two new organizations that promised well. The Patrons of Canadian Art was established to serve as a support group for the society and an enrichment for the interested layman. For several years it grew and flourished. The Professional Artists of Canada was a federation of the Royal Canadian Academy, the OSA, the Canadian Society of Painters in Water Colour, the Sculpture Society of Canada, the Graphic Artists, and the Painter-Etchers, formed in order to take a united voice to Ottawa. We presented our brief to Judy LaMarsh, then Secretary of State. I hope it was of some use in persuading the government to be more generous in its support of the arts. Afterwards the academy pulled out of the federation, and the other societies went their separate ways.

I remember one dismal press conference in Ed's office when we had invited Barrie Hale and a couple of other writers, critics or reporters, to brief them about the forthcoming exhibition of the society with what we hoped was interesting information about the new members and the works that had just won awards. Barrie sat slouched in an easy chair, put his feet on the coffee table, and buried himself in a magazine. I found myself wishing he were my student and I could teach him something about manners.

It was as president of the OSA that I volunteered to be a witness in the trial of Dorothy Cameron on a charge of obscenity. Her gallery on Yonge Street had mounted an exhibition named Eros 65, predictably full of sexual content, explicit or implicit. Certain of the works were seized by the police and held as evidence. Kildare Dobbs described the case for *Saturday Night* and reported that the police offered to drop the charge if Dorothy would remove one painting by Robert Markle. She decided to refuse, and the case went to trial. I cherish Dobbs's report of my part in that trial.

> Perhaps the most engaging witness is Miss Doris McCarthy, president of the Ontario Society of Artists and a teacher of more than thirty years' experience. Small and neat, she answers Rickaby's questions in light ladylike tones. Discussing one of the drawings, he mentions (once more) the Crown's favourite word, genitalia. Says Miss McCarthy

sweetly, "Sometimes they seem appealing to human beings."

"Do you find anything obscene?"

"No, there's nothing obscene about sex or the human body, necessarily."

Magistrate Hayes intervenes. "What do you mean by 'necessarily'?"

"I mean that sex by itself as such is not obscene." But Rickaby wants an example of the implied exception. Miss McCarthy is having none of that. "I'm *certainly* not going to stand here trying to think up something that is sexual and could be obscene!"

Meredith Fleming was counsel for the defence, with William Withrow, director of the AGO, and the critic Harry Malcolmson as two others of his witnesses. But in spite of my offering an illustrated catalogue of Picasso drawings from the AGO to demonstrate that community standards had not been violated, Dorothy lost the case. It's hard to believe how much has changed in twenty-five years.

Dobbs's comments about Robert Markle are interesting for the light they throw on the prevailing thinking about art. In the same *Saturday Night* article he wrote: "From the public straining for a glimpse of the offending exhibits, Markle and his two fellow-artists are conspicuously absent. Markle with his black leather jacket and round Mohawk face is hardly a reassuring figure. He's apt to be personally removed in a plain brown wrapper. Markle has been unlucky. He's had difficulty winning recognition from an art Establishment that cannot take figurative painting seriously. And now that he's won it, he's about to suffer because the expert witnesses drawn from the same Establishment are so deeply committed to abstract art they have no terms to defend his treatment of a subject."

Ed Parker got me into a weekly broadcast, *OSA on the Air*, which began at a Brampton station and eventually moved to CJRT. I enjoyed the broadcasts, which were a chance to interview artists, educators, administrators, and anyone else who I judged would be interesting and interested. But I was the research person, the secretary who extended the invitations and made the appointments, the interviewer, and even wrote the thank-you letters afterwards. The whole organization was my baby. No wonder I spent so much time on the telephone. For three years my life was desk and telephone at school, desk and telephone at home, and meetings, meetings, meetings.

And yet it was during those years that I was working with simplified colour-field and hard-edge painting. The OSA eased off in the summer and let me escape to Georgian Bay with Ginny, where I tried to *say* the rocks and water movements in the simplest way possible. One curious observation is that in this most hectic time of my life, my work had a serenity that was new. Perhaps it became a sanctuary for me.

Back at home, a new patio I had built was a great success, filling the angle between the porch and the big studio. I persuaded Bailey Leslie, one of the very good potters at Central Tech, to make a three-tiered fountain for it. By this time the township was delivering water and I was no longer wholly dependent on my rain-water cistern. This fountain fell into a shallow pool only three feet across, but it brought the sky right down to the patio. If a square yard of reflected sky was that good, what would a whole pond be like?

The next year I staked out a shape that started on the near side of the big apple tree, swung towards the house beside the broad path that runs to the edge of the bluffs, curved gently across the lawn, and back towards the apple tree. I would sit on the patio and imagine water inside the stakes. But I could not begin to imagine all the extra delights that the pond would bring. Now the sky is close to me, often a very different sky from the one reflected in the more distant lake. Every spring I am visited by mallards, mating, squabbling over which male can chase which other away, and later in the spring, fraternizing amicably, as many as six at a time. The big apple tree uses the pond as a mirror. In the fall I get a great blue heron, absurdly out of scale, stalking along the edge and sometimes catching a fish and tossing it about to get it pointed right for swallowing.

Almost my favourite moment of the year is the first evening in May that it is warm enough to leave the front door open at night. I lie in bed listening to the thrilling, trilling, shrilling music of the fat toads who appear by magic and leap into the pond for their mating. For several days and nights their music dominates my life. Then I see the long ribbons of eggs they have festooned across the water, and later the tadpoles that the eggs have turned into. Next come the small boys. "Please Missus, have you a jar I could put some tadpoles into?" How many of the

little black wrigglers are eaten by the birds? How many
of them grow legs and hop out and away to wait for
mating season next year?

"October 2, 1965: Too many riches to stay silent. One
of them is biting the corner of this book, purring loudly,
tramping about among the bedclothes, Graeme at seven
months. Josey has left Nick asleep in the studio and
joined us silently, her eyes enormous. The kitten has
rolled over on her back as Jo came up to my chest, and
Jo's kettle turned on. All day gusts have chased each
other across the purple water of the pond, and the asters,
the michaelmas daisies, the darkening goldenrod have
been tossed about in the wind. Sun showers pelted down
into the pond. The trees have been alive with wrens,
warblers, waxwings, every bird and his family and cousins flittering southwards."

The pond had another gift for me. December brought
a week of sharp cold that froze the surface to a tempting
smoothness. I borrowed some skates and discovered that
I hadn't quite forgotten the feeling. I soon wanted more,
and turned to the skating clubs with indoor rinks for some
instruction and the intoxicating pleasure of dancing on
skates. One memorable night Malcolm Croggon phoned
to say that Grenadier Pond, west of High Park, was sheer
ice, and I must come out. It was a brilliant, very cold night,
windless, with stars close enough to touch and street
lights too far away to spoil the darkness. We and perhaps
four other people had the freedom of that great stretch of
polished black satin. A new delight, no boundaries, no
traffic.

I have forgotten whether this was before or after I had
begun to recognize that I was falling in love with Mal-

colm. He was a great companion. We had the same tastes in radio and television. Malcolm would phone me at the end of *Masterpiece Theatre* or a special talk program on the radio to ask was I listening or watching that? Wasn't it terrific? or terrible? as the case might be. If a movie sounded specially good, we would plan to see it together. Everything we did together was doubly enjoyable, and we were together often. But he was fourteen years younger than I, and I didn't know whether he felt as I did. I had no intention of letting myself go overboard in my emotions if it wasn't mutual, and I certainly didn't want to risk losing our friendship by frightening him. The German girl he had taken out for a couple of years had faded from the picture. There was nobody else. I wondered if he wanted marriage at all. He was in his forties and I in my late fifties. Was that too much of a gap? All my friends enjoyed him, and he had become almost family to Ginny and Ed. I wondered if we might work as a pair.

One night at Fool's Paradise, listening to a Segovia record in front of the fire, I suggested that we should not see so much of each other unless we were willing to fall in love, and Malcolm made it clear that he was not willing. "So where does that leave us?" he asked. "Friends as before," I assured him. It was our last word on the subject. My enjoyment of Malcolm was unabated, and we were as close friends as it is possible to be without letting it ripen into love. But I have never since been able to enjoy classical guitar.

In the mid-sixties Virginia was appointed second assistant head of the art department. I was devastated. I had

loses seniority

been so confident of the solidarity of the team of four, Charles and Dawson and Doris and Ginny, in that order of seniority, that I experienced this as a betrayal by the two men and a personal rejection. I was willing to believe that Charles and Dawson had reasons that seemed good to them for supporting her promotion, and I knew that they would have been consulted before her appointment. I was glad, or tried to be, for Ginny, and I was sure she would be a good administrator, but why could they not have explained to me as a friend why they or the brass above them had set seniority aside? I could take honest criticism and never did think I was perfect; indeed, each of us four had special strengths and weaknesses. Ginny and I were only a year apart in age, but I had seven years' seniority. I had been administering up to my eyeballs during the OSA years, and my status as a painter was high. Why was I passed over? I didn't hold it against Ginny, but I did hold it against both Charles and Dawson that neither of them was frank enough to talk to me to prepare me for the announcement. To this day I do not know why. Perhaps I was not as easy to get along with as Virginia, more abrasive, too blunt. It doesn't seem a weighty enough reason to be the answer.

I have realized since then what a common and bitter experience it is for the middle-aged worker to have a younger person promoted over his head. I gave the party to mark Ginny's promotion and was glad that there had never been any personal resentment against her from which I had to recover. But I was so shaken that I started to think about changing my job. Perhaps the College of Art might have a place for me. Many people would assume that to be a step up. But I knew something of the politics there, and that it had never been a happy staff. There was no other secondary-school art department in Toronto in the same class as ours at Central. This was before the proliferation of community colleges, which was soon to come. However, the University of Toronto was building a campus in Scarborough. I began inquiries into the possibility that Scarborough College might need an artist on staff.

A by-product of this was a luncheon meeting with Wyn Plumptre, the principal, at Fool's Paradise, where we got to know each other a bit, discovered much in common, and I ended up forgetting about a job for me in my concern that the new college should not leave art entirely out of its program. Principal Plumptre gave me a sympathetic hearing, but it was too early for the college to set up an art department then. Scarborough College did use me for a series of evening lectures and hung an exhibition of my hard-edged paintings in the dramatic new building, topped off with a festive reception in the principal's residence. This was my first meeting with Beryl Plumptre, who was as capable and charming a hostess as she was everything else in her distinguished public career. A few years later it was in this same principal's residence that I helped celebrate their son Tim's wedding to Barbara Laskin, daughter of my darling Peggy and Bora. And time dulled the pain, as time does.

One Sunday afternoon in the spring of 1968, the mayor of Scarborough, Albert Campbell, called me. We had mutual friends, had met socially, and were on a first-name basis. Could he bring me a small problem in design? Ab turned up with some dismal little realistic sketches of Scarborough Bluffs, which he wanted if possible to incorporate into a flag for what was then the borough of Scarborough. Fortunately, Ab was an intelligent man. He understood at once my explanation of the principles of heraldry and the importance of keeping any image that is to be repeated many times simple and perfect in design. I asked for a couple of days to come up with something suitable.

When he saw my sketches, Ab agreed with my own first choice among them. I had made a repeating abstract shape for the bluffs and conventionalized the waves, both blue on a white ground, with a carefully placed red maple leaf to put our Scarborough in Canada. He took the design away to have it drawn up in finished form. A week later, when I saw how the graphics company had interpreted my sketch, I was dismayed. They had changed and spoiled the proportions and taken all the vitality out of the scallops of the waves. Once again, when I pointed this out to Ab, he could see the difference, and he took the drawing back for correction. Then he gave me a lesson in diplomacy. This was just after the great Canadian flag fight, which had almost split the country. Instead of starting that kind of controversy, he had a couple of small flags made up in silk. From time to time, when an official or politician was in his office, he would invite his guest to look at the flag and ask if it might be a good thing for the athletes to carry when they represented Scarborough in games away from home. Before it was adopted as the official Scarborough flag, it had been used a few times, everyone had seen it and approved, and his proposal sailed smoothly through.

That year, 1968, was also the year my darling Nicky
left me at just a month less than twenty-one years of age.
Poor little frail old boy, and sweet as ever. The vet exam-
ined him and gave me a grim diagnosis – teeth ok, but
bone of the jaw perished, apt to break off any time, full
of infection and possibly pain, enough reason for his not
eating. I wept all night and most of the next day at the
thought of having him put down, but I realized that I must
see it through myself before I went north and not leave
Ginty to face that. Dr. Graham agreed to come to the
house, but that night Nicky disappeared and we couldn't
find him or any trace of him. It was, to me, as if he had
loved me enough to spare me his death. Several years later
I found his skeleton under the house where he had crept
to die, and buried it under the big apple tree. For years
every time I saw a black cat my heart turned over.

cat's death

Nicky's death was the second, but by no means the last.
My brother Kenneth had moved from Toledo to Florida
shortly after a first heart attack. There he was able to
continue his work, but at a reduced pace and without the
community involvement that had been so demanding of
his time and energy. The move gave him some good years
and me a reason for visits that let me see where Ginty and
Milly spent their winters, as well as keep in close touch
with Ken. He was important to me, my big brother, who
could talk more freely to me than to anyone else in the
family and to whom I could turn for advice, for money in
an emergency, and for an eye that was perceptive about
my work. When I phoned him to tell him about Mother's
death, I said that he need not come up; Doug and I could
manage. Afterwards I realized that if I didn't need him
for any practical reason, I did need him to be with me,

and when I phoned back to say "Please come," he was already on his way.

His death was sudden and hard to accept, hard even to realize because I was accustomed to not seeing him often. Flying down to the funeral, and the scattered family coming together there, pressed home to me the value of the rituals, the centuries of experience that lie behind our conventional social patterns. Funerals are important. We need a way of externalizing our grief and sharing it.

I had plenty of grief to digest in the sixties. A few months after Expo 67, Dawson Kennedy died. Dawson couldn't die. Dawson had been there every day forever. He was Uncle Dawson to one generation of students, darling Dawson to me, friend, teacher, the foundation of the world in spite of his having done me dirt about Ginny's promotion. A cornerstone had fallen out of the art department.

Dawson's funeral was worthy of him. The large Bloor Street United Church was full. Students poured in, parking their portfolios at the door. Kathy stood there like a queen, greeting each of them by name, beautiful in the dignity of her grief. And there were even touches of comedy that seemed right. As the cortège moved slowly along Hoskin Avenue and across town on Wellesley, two police officers on motorcycles shot past us in every block to be ready to leap off their machines and stop cross-traffic at the next intersection. Dawson would have loved that.

But he was no longer there to laugh with us. The art department was empty, bereft. Being made the new assistant head was no consolation.

The next to go was Jessie Macpherson. To my generation of CGIT she had been the Big Chief, our role model,
our guru. To thousands of young women at Victoria
College and their male contemporaries she had been a
leader, responsible for the increased presence of art in
their university buildings and lives. To Marjorie she had
been a rich and constant love, in the reflection of which
I also lived. Marjorie had been overseas with Roy when
a heart attack put Jessie into hospital. There she clung to
life until Marjorie reached her bedside. Only then was
she ready to die, with her hand in Marjorie's.

Arthur Lismer died the same day, in Montreal, but he
was buried with other members of the Group of Seven at
Kleinberg, twenty-five miles north of Toronto. A gallery
to house their collection of the work of the Group of
Seven had been built by Bob and Signe McMichael and
then given to the province of Ontario. One section of the
beautiful grounds had been made into a memorial garden
in which the artists could be buried.

"April 27, 1969: Friday afternoon Charles and I drove
up to the McMichaels' and stood in a warm wind on a
sunny little hilltop, with the ghosts of my twenties, while
Casson read a eulogy on Arthur Lismer, a young priest
said words that sounded all wrong in the context, and the
ashes were lowered into the ground. Gladys Montgom-
ery, Yvonne Housser and Rody Kenny Courtice, Tilly
Cowan, Erma Lennox Sutcliffe and her sister Jean, Dorothy Medhurst, all from the same past. A.Y. Jackson was
looking really well, although his eyes were red-rimmed.
It was curiously right – although probably Arthur would
have been sardonic about it all."

The "same past" from which those women had come

was the period when Lismer had gone from being vice-principal of the Ontario College of Art to become the guiding mind of the Toronto Art Students' League, which splintered from the college when Arthur resigned. Later they had worked with him as I did, as assistants in his children's classes at the Art Gallery of Toronto before it became the AGO. We had all remained friends, although our paths seldom crossed. Thirty intervening years had not eroded our affection and respect for that eccentric, quirky, passionate, and creative genius.

Following far too closely on all of this, soon after Marjorie and Roy had returned from Europe, came her emergency operation for suspected cancer. I have forgotten the details but not the terror, and not the relief when the operation was over and I could let the tears come.

By this time I had completed my three-year term as president of the Ontario Society of Artists and, while still on the executive, was relieved of the heavy responsibility. However, I was more than ready for the sanctuary of the cottage at Georgian Bay and the convenience of the new studio there. It was an escape to peace. I was working on my Wavement series, analysing the movement of the water under different conditions of wind and light, and translating the movement into areas of flat colour.

It was the next autumn that I had a telephone call from a stranger who said that he might be interested in buying some paintings. Could he come to see me? Even the fact that my home and studio were so far from town didn't discourage him, and he turned up at the door the next night. He was a handsome young Hungarian immigrant,

one Leslie Reichel. He told me that he had found reproductions of some of my work in old OSA and RCA catalogues. Did I have any of that old work still around? It
was the twelve-by-sixteen oil panels that he was interested in, and the big cabinet in my studio was full of them.
It was a pleasure to get them out and show them. All the
sketches I had kept were good ones, paintings that I had
considered too successful to clear out just to make more
space. Leslie picked not one but six, and I was glad to
agree on a cut rate for quantity. I think it was about thirty
dollars each, and he paid cash. I was so surprised that I
even wondered if there might be something shady about
the deal. But he sounded all right. He was working in a
framing shop uptown and told me that he intended to
frame them well and sell them. Good for him, I thought.

This was just the beginning. Within a few days he was
back for twenty more, and eventually he had almost forty
of my best old panels. A few weeks later he had framed
them all, beautifully, rented the Gutenberg Gallery on
Yonge Street, and was advertising an exhibition of the
work of DORIS McCARTHY. I went to see the show and
was delighted with it. The gallery was well hung, with a
single row of paintings, not crowded, and by the time I
got there in the second week more than half were sporting
red spots. What was more, they were priced at a hundred
and eighty-five dollars each, more than I would ever have
dared to ask. Leslie's profit pleased me as much as the
look of the work.

Three-quarters of the show was sold by the time it
closed, but all the paintings left were bought by another
art dealer whose basic business was in antiques. A few
years later they were on view in his shop, and the price

had jumped to a thousand dollars. I considered this both gratifying and amusing. They wouldn't sell at that sum, of course, but it was a satisfaction to see the price tags. I considered it to be good advertising.

Leslie was the first art dealer who had ever let me know that he thought my work had quality and was worth promoting. My appreciation of his encouragement was the beginning of a friendship that has outlasted any professional involvement.

The autumn of the Gutenberg show, Ginny and Yvonne and I heard rumours that Jacknife Lodge next to us at Georgian Bay was to be sold. Vince Thomas, who had built it and run it, was an artist himself and had through the years attracted many painters as guests. Gordon Webber had lived for months in the little cottage at the end of the point. Goodridge Roberts had spent a summer there (and had taken Vince's wife with him when he left). Jacques de Tonnancour had painted from our peninsula. Barker Fairley was a regular visitor. Vincent had been a good neighbour, and any suggestion of a change worried us. All the buildings were out of sight, but our view included his long point, which swept from wave-washed bare rock at the far end up to the high granite hill behind us. There were clumps of noble pines and scrubby oak. What if it were sold and someone built a cottage that would overlook us? Goodbye precious privacy. We had explored the shore edge and climbed to the high point as our evening walk for years. A new owner might not be so hospitable.

Yvonne and I phoned Vince's home in Port Hope to set up a date, and one wintry Saturday morning drove down there together to see if we could negotiate a purchase. In

conference with Ginny we had worked out the figure we
could manage to pay. We looked suitably shocked when
he mentioned how much he would have to ask, but it was
exactly what we were prepared for, and by the time we
left we had shaken hands on it and promised to meet him
up at the bay to stake out the piece that we were buying.

We gathered up there one sparkling January morning
and scrambled about through the snow, locating the old
boundary markers, drawing new lines. For us one thrill
was discovering that we already owned the high granite
hill that we had always assumed belonged to the Jacknife
property. The other was the realization that Gordon
Webber's little cabin was on our new piece. There was a
great celebration when we got back to report to Ginny.

We talked about the little cottage, tempted to embrace
it and keep it, but that would give us three buildings to
maintain when even two ate into the painting time. Then
we cooked up the idea of offering it to Flo and her sister
Mary to have for their own. Since we were not allowed
to divide the property, we brought Mary into partnership
in the land but still let them have sole ownership of the
cottage. The next summer I had the delight of remodelling
the building, transforming it from a double cabin designed for sleeping only to a complete cottage. I took out
the centre partition wall and used the two-by-fours from
it to make tie-beams to strengthen the roof. I measured
and drew and pried apart and sawed and hammered.
Ginny and Flo picked up and swept and stained and
sewed and went to town to shop. Mary had short holidays, and our objective was to have the cottage finished
by the time she came. We made the deadline with only
hours to spare.

This was the summer that a beaver dropped a tree on Flo's old Chev, and stove in the roof and trunk. That was funny enough, but on her way out to the Snug Harbour marina to get expert advice and a repair job, Flo drove into a pot-hole and there was a report like a gunshot. At the marina she discovered that the dent had popped out again. Emergency over.

The next spring, when I was ready for a one-man show, I approached Carl Gutenberg myself, and he was happy to give me his gallery on the usual basis of a commission on sales, 40 per cent. Leslie had paid two hundred dollars' rent instead of a commission, and Carl had learned by the experience.

"June 7, 1971: I've had more reaction from this show than from any exhibition I've ever given. Kay Kritzwiser's column in the *Globe and Mail* was warm and enthusiastic. It's nice. I am so grateful to Leslie for believing in my stuff and actually working like a salesman. It's marvellous after all these years to have it demonstrated that they are worth real money to some people. They are selling at $150.00 or $160.00 and going quickly. I begin to imagine how Alan Collier and Adrian Dingle and so on have felt these years when their paintings were sold out the first night. Leslie started it all off well by putting six of them in Sotheby's May sale for me, paying for good big reproductions and being lucky enough to draw a good position in the catalogue. They fetched from $210.00 to $325.00 there with no pump priming."

A few weeks later I sold forty-three old sketches to Kristiansen, who owned a gallery out in Vancouver, the Art Emporium, per Leslie. "Now I have a wad of fifty-six twenty-dollar bills, four fifties, and four hundreds, the most paper money I've ever seen, stuffed in an envelope waiting to be dropped into the bank tomorrow. I'm really delighted to clear them out and to realize that they will be in circulation, but there are some priceless memories wrapped in them, especially the North Lake sketches, some learning too, and some good hard painting."

A few months later Mr. Kristiansen was in town himself and asked me to bring more of the small oil panels in to the school to let him see them. He walked away with another bundle, which just about cleaned me out of the sketches of the thirties and forties.

By this time Charlie Goldhamer had retired and Ginny was head of the department, with me as her senior assistant. We were a comfortable team, able to work side by side in the office as smoothly as we had worked side by side at the Gaspé and at the cottage for so many years. I had the personal satisfaction at long last of being allowed to do the timetables, which became like a large and complicated game of Scrabble, with an almost infinite variety of possibilities and with every class and teacher needing some special considerations, which I enjoyed trying to satisfy.

Once I was freed of the OSA responsibility I had used my spare periods to enrol in the weaving class, and after I had a loom at home and enough experience to be able to weave on my own, I moved to Andrew Fussel's metalwork class. This was a new world. It had never occurred to me that metal was malleable and that a mere amateur could make things with it. Bliss was to cut a circle out of a flat piece of heavy aluminum, lay it over a chunk of wood with a hollow in it, and bash away with a hard rubber mallet, watching it gradually take shape under the blows and curling into the very form I had intended. I think the special charm was that it was such physical work, a complete rest from coping with human relations and making decisions.

I had by this time recovered the sense of bodily well-being that I had lost for the whole ten years of the menopause. I was still tired out by the end of a teaching day, but at least I could start each morning full of energy and enthusiasm. And I had begun the countdown to 1972, which would be the end of the tunnel.

Virginia Luz and Doris relishing their wonderful year, 1951.

Ginny, Dino,
and Doris
in Venice,
January
1951.

Margaret Cork and
Nicky at home at
Fool's Paradise.

The beginning of a long love affair with Stratford: Ginny, Flo, Doris and Nan.

Jennie McCarthy and Tammy, two aging ladies.

DM4, my classroom with the new stands for still life; Kathleen Fekete at work.

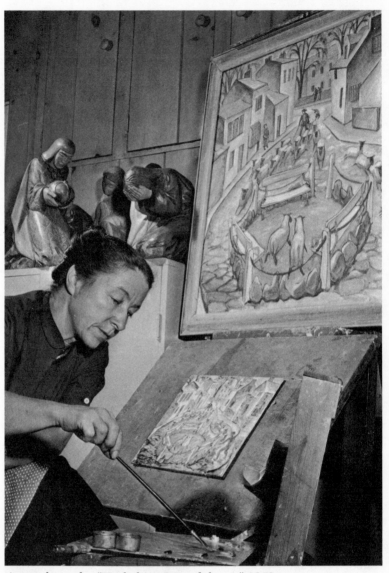

At work on the "Yorkshire Roundabout," 1952.

Peter and Bobs Haworth, Jocelyn Taylor, and Ginny take a lunch break during a Thanksgiving painting weekend, 1962.

A party at Fool's Paradise. Back row: Ginny Luz, Herman Voaden, Violet Voaden, George McMurtry, Dawson Kennedy; front row: Bobs Haworth, Kathleen Kennedy, Yvonne McKague Housser.

Ginny at work above Sanctuary Lake, Haliburton,
October 1966.

Pearl McGinnis –
"Ginty" – with
Josie, 1968.

Jocelyn Taylor and Doris with Dr. Boyd Neel at the gala
opening in Hamilton of the juried exhibition of the Canadian
Society of Painters in Water Colour, 1957.

Malcolm Croggon
with Josie, 1966.

The Tamaki
garden supper,
Kyoto, Japan,
1961.

Christmas Eve
in Bethlehem,
1961.

Dino, *c.* 1965.

Marjorie and Doris
together in Rome,
1962.

Dressed to make her debut as the first woman president of the Ontario Society of Artists, Canada's senior professional art society, 1966.

Marjorie and Doris at Fool's Paradise.

A detail from *The Wedding at Cana in Galilee*, the hanging at Cana Place, Scarborough.

Carved crêche figures at the Church of St. Aidan, Toronto.

5

Arctic Awakening

MY LAST FEW YEARS of teaching were so pleasant that the tunnel began to feel more like an arcade with a glass roof that let some sunshine in. Ginny and I enjoyed working together. In the office at adjoining desks we sat side by side under the skylight with our backs to the windows, a spider plant spilling its graceful branches above us. Low bookcases down each side of the room were full of good art books and served as stands for display pieces of pottery and sculpture made by the students. Above them were hung framed examples of students' drawings and paintings. It was a gracious office, with comfortable chairs for visitors, and staff and students flowed in and out freely. We worked to music. But I had looked forward to retirement for so long as my opportunity to be at last a full-time artist that when the time came I cast few backward glances. After all, Ginny and I were partners

at Georgian Bay, with every summer ahead of us to live
and work together.

A younger woman who had joined the art department
staff after our move to the new building was Barbara
Greene. She relieved Ginny of some of her illustration
classes and shared still life with me. She was a water-
colourist, allergic to turps, which made my classroom sometimes pretty tough for her to work in. She was also a
compulsive gardener, and when I told her about a cottage
for rent close to me on the edge of the bluffs that had a whole
acre of orchard, she became my neighbour. We drove to and
from school together, swapped garden produce, and became good friends. It was Barbara who shared with Malcolm and Boyd the party of the cat in the fireplace. She was
also an adventurer and had made her own solitary trek
around the world, just months before I did.

I have forgotten which was the chicken and which the
egg, but between us we hatched a plan to go up to the
high Arctic in the summer of 1972 and paint there. Dalton
Muir, Fran Dalziel's brother-in-law, was Ottawa's eco-
logical watch-dog in the north at this time, monitoring the
effects on the country of development by the mining and
oil companies. He was glad to give us a session with his
superb slides of the landscape, the flowers, the ice formations, the wildlife, and the settlements. He knew them all
intimately and loved them passionately. On the basis of
what he showed us, we decided to make Pond Inlet our
headquarters. It is a settlement on the north side of Baffin
Island and looks across a forty-mile strait to Bylot Island,
which lies like a stage set of mountains and glaciers.
Dalton's photographs were irresistible.

I wrote to the rector of the Anglican church there,

asking about accommodation and explaining our needs.
Weeks went by; then a letter came from John Scullion,
the settlement manager, explaining that the minister had
been leaving for England and had turned over our inquiry
to him. Could we make do with staying in the kindergarten and using the teachers' living quarters? The writer
Sheila Burnford (author of *The Incredible Journey*) and the
artist Susan Ross had used it the previous summer and
found it satisfactory. Please let him know what day we
expected to arrive.

While we were still working on those details, one of my
adult students remembered reading about a trip organized by the Federation of Ontario Naturalists for seven
days' exploration of the wildlife of the Arctic, with Resolute Bay as its base. We telephoned immediately and
were lucky enough to book the last two places in the
group that left after the end of school term. That meant a
week to acquire a bird's-eye view of the Arctic before we
settled in to paint in one place.

We planned in careful detail what to take, what to
wear, how to handle our art supplies when all transport
was by air or by foot. Barbara chose water-colour, but I
wanted to work in oil. I designed a light aluminum shipping crate with balsa-wood strips inside to separate the
wet panels, and asked Andrew Fussel about obtaining the
aluminum. Dear Andrew took my drawing, to be sure of
the size of everything, and came back after a weekend
with the crate completely made as a surprise present for
me. It will carry forty panels, enough for three weeks on
the job.

I had begun teaching in 1932, and after forty years one
could retire with full pension, even if not yet sixty-five

years old. And my retirement gratuity would more than
cover the cost of the Arctic trip.

That June is memorable. The field in front of the house
had grown high before the hay was cut. Wind rippled it
into waves and blew the petals from the apple trees like
confetti into the pond. Fool's Paradise was at its loveliest.
But there was an irony for me in its beauty and in the
reality of the retirement to which I had looked forward
for so long. At my routine medical check-up early in the
month, Paul Pitt, my doctor and friend, had observed a
lump in my neck that he decided should be X-rayed. Next
morning the technicians up at the lab did their stuff, and
then did it again with a couple of extra bodies in atten-
dance. I began to suspect that they had hit pay dirt. My
suspicions were confirmed when Paul phoned that very
afternoon with the news that an operation was advisable.
He assured me that it was not an emergency and could
wait until I came back from the Arctic. I can still feel the
rake in my hand and smell the new hay as I gathered it
into piles to carry back to the garden for mulch, wondering if my freedom was to be over in a few months, and I
dead of cancer. Why not I? Life had been very good to
me, and it seemed reasonable that there should be my
share of trouble waiting.

I have never regretted that cancer scare. It was not the
first time I had faced the possibility. But on the earlier
occasion I was much younger, not nearly so happy, still
with twenty gruelling years of work ahead of me and
accustomed to bracing myself to accept whatever came,
grateful when it turned out to be not too bad. This time
it was a reminder that life even at its most idyllic is fragile.
I carry that reminder with me now. I feel immortal,

less tolerable of waste

vigorous, full of pleasure in today and alluring plans for tomorrow. But as I move into my eighties I realize that the time ahead grows shorter and shorter. Every good hour is doubly precious, and I am even less able to tolerate wasting any of it.

In early summer, when I joined Ginny at the cottage after the operation and told her that the surgeon had removed part of the thyroid, her comment was a typical family remark, compounded equally of affection and irony. "It will perhaps cut you down to normal."

"July 5, 1972: Left FP by taxi for a serene (physically) flight to Montreal after a two-hour session on a perfect morning from 6:00 A.M. to 8:00 A.M. raking the last southern corner of the hayfield and finishing the strip east of the long walk. I raked and raked, analysing my feelings and recognizing that my strongest emotion in the face of this Arctic trip was apprehension, afraid as usual of the painting, afraid of doing tedious sketches, afraid of the opinions of the others on the trip, afraid of Barbara (I can't imagine why), afraid of forgetting essential equipment, afraid of the overweight baggage bill, afraid of the confusion of too much luggage. I couldn't claim to be excited at all, just tense."

But as soon as I had shoved the bags and the unwieldy crate into the lockers at Dorval and found myself with my hands free, on the bus to Montreal, my spirits began to soar, and I knew all the delicious excitement of the good days of 1961 and 1962. I was travelling again, and being in Montreal was an adventure.

The next morning Barbara and I were waiting in the

air terminal at Dorval, trying to guess who among the large men in plaid shirts and women in sturdy boots and slacks were to be our fellow naturalists, when one of us discovered that the rather vague-looking woman in glasses wearing a skirt and sweater was also bound for Resolute Bay. Her home was South Carolina, and no, she was not one of our party. Was she going on business or pleasure? In curiosity, really. In her gentle southern voice she explained that she had never been north before and she was planning to live with an Eskimo family and see something of the authentic life of the Arctic. Her children were old enough to leave behind and her husband was not free to come. But her luggage had gone astray somewhere between South Carolina and Montreal, and she was having to go on without it in the hope that it would be sent after her.

Teachers are compulsive Samaritans. We were concerned about how she would survive in the north until the luggage arrived, and invited her to stay close to us and share whatever we could spare from our gear when we unpacked. Roberta Crittenden, as we learned she was, became our charge, our entertainment, and our friend. Most of the time she lived with an Inuit family about three miles from the hotel that housed the naturalists, having bought boots and jacket at the local Hudson's Bay store and borrowed a sleeping bag from an oilman who was off home. Our party produced extra sweaters, slacks, and other essentials. We saw her often, wistfully looking for the wandering bags, always in vain. When we were ready to fly over to Pond Inlet, she came with us and lived with us in the kindergarten.

The Resolute hotel had been contrived from a series of

quonset huts, joined together to provide accommodation for the employees of the oil companies, mines, research teams, and travellers on government business. The food was astonishing, both in quality and quantity: roast beef, turkey, fresh Arctic char, all the salads we could wish, pies and cakes in abundance, and good coffee available any time in the lobby. Service was simple, cafeteria style, and the dining-room was stark but clean. For atmosphere you went to the Arctic Club Bar, where there was enough noise and tobacco smoke to give anyone the illusion of having a good time. The hotel was normally an all-male domain, but in deference to us naturalists one of the washrooms had a temporary "Ladies" sign taped on the door.

Outside the hotel Resolute was one wide gravel main street between two rows of orange huts of various shapes and bulks, with a group of turquoise huts cutting off the view at one end of the street and Resolute Bay Observatory, on the sea flats, the focus of attention at the other. This Resolute was nothing but a transient centre. The real village, where Roberta was staying, was a couple of miles away, strung along a shingle beach. It was a long arc of shacks and small pre-fab houses of one or two rooms, each surrounded by an incredible litter of snowmobiles, rough hand-made cargo sleds, sealskins stretched on racks to dry, oil barrels, gasoline tins, abandoned mittens, scarves, boots, Coke bottles, dead dogs and seal carcasses left to lie, scrap plywood, and plastic. I was shocked by what looked to me like dirt and confusion.

All Inuit villages at this time were in a state of transition from the traditional temporary tent settlements to something more permanent and comfortable. When the gov-

ernment authorities decided to educate the Inuit children
and insisted that they all attend school every winter, they
built schools and boarding-houses where a house mother
and father could look after the children while the grown-
ups were off in winter camp. But Eskimo parents were
not willing to leave their children. They set up their tents
near the school for the winter, and eventually the government flew in houses for them that were essentially good
wooden tents, little one-room slope-sided houses that
were all over the settlements in 1972. They were weather-
tight and equipped with stoves, eventually even with
electricity. But they were very small, with no storage
space. The tradition had been to move camp several times
a year, abandoning the refuse, taking only what could be
loaded on a sled and pulled by the family's dog-team. With
permanent homes had come possessions – radios, chairs
and tables, bicycles – and no place to store them except
on the roof or on the ground beside the house. The new
practice was for every village to have one great day of
clean-up after the snow had melted and exposed the
garbage. The school laid in a supply of green garbage bags
and sent all the children out harvesting, with prizes for
the ones who filled the most bags.

On our first night in the Arctic (night by courtesy; it
never did get dark) we were gathered in the hotel lounge
to be given an outline of our program for the next day and
what turned out to be the best advice possible: "Hang
loose." We remembered it often when the plane couldn't
take off as scheduled because of fog, or when rain can-
celled the planned walk to watch the deep-sea divers.

"Resolute Bay, July 8, 1972: What a sixty-second
birthday, completely forgotten until now, lying in my

sleeping-bag on a gaudy sun-cot in the cook-tent of the Stuart MacDonald–Bathurst Island research station, recalling the adventures of the day before and thinking back over the paintings I had done, and dating them. That's when I realized that it was on my birthday that I had fallen into Sanderling Creek, some fifteen miles from the magnetic north pole, when I had left the bird-watchers and decided to return home to do a sketch. The snow on my side of the creek felt reasonably firm and seemed fairly shallow. The stream was rushing, green, deep enough but narrow. The other side looked worth a try. But the jump broke through into a foot and a half of water, and the next frantic step flung me even deeper and pinned me there, with the ice water pouring into my boots. I pulled myself out by kneeling on my slicker so that I wouldn't fall still further in, and stood on it to get my balance again before jumping back to the side I had just left, remembering too late Gerry McKeating's warnings, 'Caution' and 'Patience.' After I had wrung out my socks and emptied my shoes twice, I slogged through mud, through water, over saxifrage hummocks, careless of moss clumps or willow patches, through snow, over ice, as fast as I could go up the long slope to the tiny beacon of the new lab building on the skyline. I kept thinking of the 'poor bloody infantry' and the way the men in the First World War went for days and weeks in wet feet and muddy clothes."

The Twin Otter that had dropped us on Bathurst Island in the morning for a day of hiking and birding was due back about four o'clock to pick us up, but it failed to appear. Hang loose. There were about four men resident at the station in limited quarters. They gallantly shared their food that evening and managed to find a few cots and mattresses. While we were waiting around for the aircraft to rescue us in the morning, a pair of eider ducks put on a floor show for us. "Father picked a nesting site and lured mother into it. She squatted in it, trying it for size or whatever else is important to a nesting eider. Not good enough. She waddled away, and father tried a new spot. Repeat of performance. After she had gone almost the complete circle of the camp, about fifty feet off, she finally approved one hollow, raked bits of stuff into it to make a nest, laid her egg, wagged her tail in satisfaction, and then we all saw the Thayer's gull watching, hovering, hoping for a meal when she should leave the nest. One of the naturalists, Stewart MacDonald, went down to the cook-tent to get food to lure the gull. Pierre, the lanky research assistant who had lent me dry boots the day before, kept his telescope trained on the duck and her egg and made notes of the time. The FON stood around in groups enjoying the drama, and the aircraft eventually sailed in, much to Gerry's relief, with assurances from the pilot that they had tried to get to us the night before but had been turned back by fog."

Twin Otters are small aircraft, able to carry only sixteen passengers. They can be fitted with soft balloon tires that allow them to land anywhere that is free of boulders. In the winter they usually wear skis, and a stretch of sea ice is kept ploughed for a landing strip. Barbara and I liked the front seats, which had the great advantage of letting us watch the controls. On the way home from Bathurst Island the pilot spotted a polar bear and flew only a few feet above him. He lolloped across the ice and slid into the sea, and we watched him pale green through the water as he swam along under the surface.

The next day we flew still farther north to Eureka, a
weather station half-way up Ellesmere Island. After the
wilderness of glacier-wrapped mountain peaks that we
had to pass over to get there, Eureka seemed hospitable,
a couple of sheds and some bright tents in a sandy hollow
among dark mountains. Eureka is where the long-tailed
jaegers are so tame they will take food from your hand.
They are handsome black birds, like crows with long
graceful double tails, and were flying around our heads
after bread bits like the pigeons in a city square. While
we were feeding the birds, who should appear but Dalton
Muir. We had a joyful reunion and were able to report
our delight with the results of the advice and help he had
given us. And while I was sitting on the ground in the
shelter of a tent, making an oil sketch, one of the lads who
came to look over my shoulder asked me if I knew Alan
Collier. Astonishing to find two human contacts at the top
of the world.

Flying home over Axel Heiberg Island, we could see
only the black jagged tips of the mountains, crooked
spines that twisted here and there above the voluptuous
billows of snow and glacier. The snow-covered mountains
from above reminded me vividly of a relief map that has
had white plaster poured over it.

The challenge that first week was to find painting
material wherever we were put down, or whenever we
were left waiting for the summons to the airfield. Besides
looking, I listened. Item: In the north you must be careful
drinking alcohol because it can be so cold and still *liquid*
that you could freeze your throat. I don't remember
where I picked up that gem of wisdom. Item: Outside the
bar a sign read

ARCTIC CLUB BAR
Admission to Members only
Membership Tickets available
on request from Barman

Hours and hours of our precious week were spent
dashing to the airport to catch the early flight to somewhere, trailing back to the hotel because the weather had
closed in, getting ready to walk in the other direction to
watch the divers at a local research station, and then
grabbing gear and running again back to the airport
because the fog had suddenly lifted. Hang loose. We were
well brainwashed. I heard never a murmur of complaint.

One of our sudden take-offs was a flight to Grise Fiord,
the most northerly of Canada's settlements. (Eureka and
Alert don't count, because they are not proper villages.)
A few years later I returned to Grise in April, which was
deep winter, a white world. This brief summer visit was
very different, with flowers everywhere, apparently
growing out of bare rock, and a big open pond in the
middle of the settlement. In the evening we were entertained by the resident engineer and his wife in one of the
two-storey "hung-basement" pre-fabs. These houses are
designed like conventional middle-class city homes, but
perched on posts, with the wind free to blow underneath.
It would be disastrous to set a house close to the ground
or on it in case heat from the house might melt the
permafrost and allow the foundation posts to sag or
collapse. You enter one of these houses by what would be
the cellar and go upstairs to the living-room, kitchen, and
bedrooms.

At the end of the week we parted with our fellow

naturalists with regret but with a real eagerness to get to
Pond Inlet and concentrated work. On the flight to Pond
the Twin Otter touched down at Arctic Bay, another
small community on Baffin Island. Barbara and I strolled
about on the airstrip and took some snapshots of such
spectacularly beautiful cloud formations and light on far
hills that I couldn't forget Arctic Bay, and succeeded in
returning there for a month three years later.

At Pond Inlet we were landed on a hill above the settlement, which lay on the shore of Lancaster Sound, a wide
stretch of ice-bound sea. Beyond the frozen sound was a
backdrop of blue-grey mountains streaked with snow and
separated by glaciers stretching right down to the sea.

The good-looking dark-haired man with the broad
shoulders and big smile who came to meet us was John
Scullion, and the little woman with the Irish face under
short red-gold hair was Colly, his wife. Because it was
already too late to shop at the Hudson's Bay store, Colly
had brought us a loaf of home-made bread, some butter,
and other emergency rations. John loaded us and our
luggage into a sort of van on caterpillar treads and drove
us down to our quarters.

We couldn't believe the space in the kindergarten –
two big classrooms, two bedrooms and a dormitory, three
bathrooms and a kitchen. Barbara and I elected to share
the bedroom that looked out to sea, and gave Roberta the
other teacher's room. One classroom was a superb studio,
with good light and all the kindergarten furniture to play
with. We had a cistern of hot water and every convenience except a flush toilet. Pond Inlet was on "honey

bags," the Arctic name for the green garbage bags used to line the toilets. Every morning a lad comes into your house without knocking, twists up the bag and takes off with it, leaving a fresh one on the floor for you to fit into place.

We soon got used to that. More disconcerting was having a strange young man walk in with his towel over his arm and disappear into the bathroom to take a bath. Some of the Inuit women would drop in, sit at the table in silence, accept a cup of tea and whatever we could find to offer with it, and after ten minutes, half an hour, or even longer, leave in the same silence. We sensed that the kindergarten had been something of a community centre, and we tried to be as pleasant as we knew how without the language. Roberta was a genius with children and gathered them about her by some strange magic independent of words. Barbara and I wanted to work, and depended on Roberta to cope with the social life. Except with the Scullions. Colly and John were so congenial, so hospitable, so generous, and so genuinely interested in what we were doing that they soon became our friends.

We were in twenty-four-hour daylight, and without the clouds and rain that had dogged us at Resolute. The hotel there had been designed for winter protection and had few windows, all of them above eye-level. My window here was on bed-level. I have always cared fanatically about seeing *out*, and this was heaven. I looked north, and as day waned the sun swung lower in the sky, crossing behind the mountains of Bylot before it climbed up to the zenith of its noon height. From my bed I had a constantly changing panorama of broken sea ice, with long cracks of dark green breaking it into patterns, the sun catching the edges of the floes in the evening and

again in the early morning, the mountain backdrop of
Bylot Island constantly changing as the light moved.

The Inuit don't follow our pattern of bed all night and
up all day. They sleep when they are tired, eat when
hungry, and so at any hour of the day or night there were
children playing outside, guns being shot, skidoos rev-
ving up and roaring around on the ice, and, best of all, the
dog chorus. That wild outcry is the very voice of the
Arctic. One husky starts to keen. It is a song, nothing like
a bark. A second chimes in, always at a different pitch,
then a third, and more and more, with often a high
soprano doing a descant that is very comic indeed.

I spent much of my painting time along the edge of the
shore, where there were storage sheds for the fishing and
hunting gear, where the dogs were tethered, and where I
could study the fantastic shapes of the ice floes and the
pressure ice.

Pressure ice is an endless delight. Every time the tide
comes in, the sea ice is pushed up. Sometimes it cracks
and breaks into pieces. Huge cakes of ice are left on edge
and frozen into position. The tide as it goes out lets some
of these broken floes sag against each other and freeze
together in jagged clusters, with fresh snow drifting about
them in scarves. All along the shore is a tumult of ice
forms, an invitation to creative design.

And when I looked up from all this foreground excitement I was looking at Bylot Island, with the pyramidal
mountains echoing the triangular shapes of the near ice
and the glaciers garlanding them in much the same way
as trails of drifted snow draped around the shore ice.

Up on the hill beside the kindergarten I had a foreground of rounded meadow with green and straw-

coloured grasses and smooth boulders covered with li-
chens of grey, grey-green, and orange. Once when I was
sitting in the heather on the moors, painting with my
sketch-box between my legs and my own shadow blocking the sun from my work, I noticed an extension on the
shadow of my head and recognized it as a bird shape.
Then I could feel little feet moving about. I sat still and
had a good sight of the horned lark when he hopped down
and looked for better forage just beyond me.

One day John Scullion organized for us a trip by
dog-sled up Navy Board Inlet, which separated us from
Bylot Island, to visit the iceberg that had been trapped by
freeze-up the year before. Colly came with us, and we
four women and John, the Inuit driver, took off for a
ten-mile scramble westward along the sea ice. The komatik, or sled, was about twelve feet long, made of heavy
wooden runners with cross-slats lashed on so that there
would be a certain amount of give. The two runners could
rise and fall over the rough sea ice almost independently.
The dogs seemed small to be pulling that heavy sled with
four women, and sometimes John too, but they ran in and
out among the lumps of sea ice, pulling sturdily and
making quite good progress. One of them, a bitch, ran
along one side with her rein usually slack, enjoying the
trip but making sure she was not doing much of the work.
It was almost mid-July by this time, and cracks were
appearing all over the ice. Narrow ones were fun and
exciting as the sled splashed across. But there was one
too wide to cross, which meant a long detour of five miles
to a place where the komatik could span it.

It was almost noon before we reached the berg. This

was the first time I had seen the brilliant turquoise and incredible green of the deep crevasses of glacial ice, the result of the enormous pressure of the weight of that great depth of ice, fifteen metres of it visible and more than ten times that depth below the surface. Microscopic organisms that live in ice can add colour too.

After lunch John attacked the berg with an axe and hacked off a good-sized chunk to take back home. Colly explained that iceberg water made the very best tea, much prized by all the locals. John lashed it on to the komatik behind the others, and I travelled home backwards, leaning against it. I missed the fun of watching the dogs, but I had the full benefit of the glories of the sunlit iceberg as we left it farther and farther behind. Therefore I had no warning when suddenly I was shoved off the sled and left sitting in a turquoise puddle. The ice had melted enough to slacken the rope. Much hilarity all round – the dogs were halted, and I ran to catch up. Lancaster Sound is a very big place to be stranded with no company but a distant iceberg.

Barbara was a good companion and a wizard of a chef, happy in the kitchen and with little welcome for anyone else there. Roberta drifted in for her meals long after Barbara and I were finished and eager to be off again painting. We accepted her assurances that she was glad to do the washing up, and left her to it.

On our last day at Pond we hung an exhibition of our work and invited people to drop in to see their world through our eyes. We offered John and Colly their choice of a thank-you gift from each of us, and John decided that he also had to have my sketch of his boat, the *Lemon*, thus beginning that summer the largest privately owned collection of McCarthy paintings extant.

The very best part of my return home was to rediscover night. After all that sunlight, how beautiful I found the darkness and the stars. Sometime I should like to experience the Arctic winter, which is long and complete and colder than anything I have ever known. But it is apparently also very beautiful, with spectacular displays of northern lights, moon and stars to dramatize the forms, and the many voices of the wind behind the keening of the dogs.

That fall I made prints of the Arctic icebergs to use as Christmas cards. June Bird, one of my old students, who was a print-maker with her own press and a generous heart, taught me how to make a block using successive layers of cardboard. Printers' ink is the consistency of a stiff ointment, and one rolls it out on a piece of glass with a gelatin roller to get it evenly thin, and then gently over the block. The ink roller misses any hollows you have cut, and the gutters beside each layer as well, which creates pleasant white outlines in the design. It was comparatively easy to control the placing of a second colour, and occasionally to blend two colours in an area. I used green and then yellow. June showed me how to print by lowering dampened paper carefully on to the block and padding it with a blanket before it was run through the press. Peeling off the paper was an exciting moment, revealing for the first time what I really had. No two inkings were identical, so that every pressing gave slightly different results, but the blocks were well enough designed that all the prints turned out to be interesting and to say something about icebergs. I think this was the germ of the iceberg fantasies that have been emerging in my work ever since.

In November I had a second show at the Gutenberg. This time it was all Arctic sketches and the Arctic canvases completed during the summer at the cottage.

"December 6, 1972: Final score out of fifty-six paintings: three kept on consignment, fifteen returned to me, thirty-eight sold, plus the two that Carl and his sister bought the night they came out for dinner. And now that the income-tax boys have caught up with me and I've come clean, although not yet assessed and paid up, the slight alarm at making so much money is also removed. They will tax it cheerfully away. A sweet young accountant, looking like a character from a Victorian romantic novel, has been vetting me. I can't not like him, and it takes much of the curse out of the process."

When the first phone call came, "This is Revenue Canada speaking," I had assumed it was one of my friends being funny, and I just laughed and hung up. When he phoned again, I told him to write to me on official paper, and when he did, I began to take him seriously. I had never declared art income nor claimed art expenses, knowing that all through the years it had cost me money to be an artist. But that was before Leslie discovered me. The character from a Victorian romantic novel had just started working for the income-tax department. I was his first assignment, and he was zealous. I turned over all my books to him. I had kept careful track through the years of any money that had come to me from the sale of my paintings, but not of my expenses. I found a few big

framing bills, but nothing else. He insisted that from now
on I must do accrual bookkeeping, which sounded to me
as if my precious freedom was to be spent struggling with
figures for the government. I paid what was demanded,
for as many years back as he asked, and found myself an
accountant to keep track of me in the future. At least I
ended up with a vendor's permit, and can now buy my
paints and canvases without provincial sales tax.

This was at the time of the oil shortage, when the price
of fuel had zoomed up and everyone was suddenly very
energy-conscious. The pine-board ceiling of my living-
room had a backing of a mere half-inch of ten-test under
the shingles, useless as insulation. It was a traumatic
decision to cover those beautiful pine boards. For six
gruelling but blissful days I cut two-inch styrofoam bats
into careful thirds, shaped the end of one third, and
painted the pieces a dirty green, which became pale
viridian when put against the warm brown of the ceiling
beams. Then I rented a ten-foot step-ladder and for five
more days climbed up and down it, balanced gingerly on
the high step and its shelf, straining to reach the peak of
the ceiling. I fitted the bats between the beams, cut thin
strips to fill any cracks that were left, laid quarter-round
to mask the joints, poked cove moulding up into the very
angle of the ridge, and held it there with a nail that I could
neither see to aim at nor reach to hold in position nor hit
because of the very narrow angle between ridge-board
and ceiling. "But it's done," I wrote triumphantly, "and it
will stop the heat pouring right through the roof." It was
such experiences of caring for my home and keeping it in
repair that made me look wryly at the friends who would
drive out some gorgeous Sunday afternoon for tea, walk

with me about the garden, and tell me how lucky I was to have such a beautiful place.

That year, 1973, the Scullions were transferred from Pond Inlet to Cape Dorset and invited the three kindergarten artists to stay with them there to paint. Cape Dorset is on the south side of Baffin Island, its hills lower and rounder than the mountains near Pond. Roberta came again, and she and I lived with the Scullions in one of the "hung basements." Its windows commanded a view over the northern half of the village and the dramatic hill behind it. Besides Roberta and me, Colly had Nick in the house that week, the government carpenter whose schedule at last allowed him to cut a big new window in her kitchen and make other overdue revisions to the house. Colly and John accepted all the inevitable chaos with serenity, and without ever making us feel that we were the last straws.

They organized our next steps, first to Frobisher Bay, where we would have to stay overnight. Joan and Gerry Morgan put us up there for the night. He was superintendent of the engineers in the Arctic, responsible for the continuing maintenance of the electrical systems and water supplies in the settlements. Joan was Colly's close friend, tall where Colly was tiny, brown where Colly was red-gold, but matching her in tolerance and warm hospitality. I enjoyed that hospitality many times during the next ten years. It was Gerry, big smiling Gerry, who loaded all our stuff into his truck and took us to the airport the next morning to catch the Twin Otter to Pangnirtung.

Pangnirtung is also on the south side of Baffin Island, part way up a narrow fiord that twists its way north among high rugged mountains. There, as a result of

Colly's intercessions, we were given permission to sleep in the kitchen of the Anglican Sunday school hall and use its stove. Dear Margaret Gardener, the priest's wife, even lent us mattresses. The only proviso was that on Sundays we should vacate the hall and leave it to the church school.

The painting was terrific here too. Twice a day at Pangnirtung the tide came in, bringing with it a flotilla of ice floes that sailed up the fiord like a regatta of small bergs. As the tide ebbed, they went back to sea, their restless movement keeping me in a constant state of excitement. I came home with enough work for another exhibition of water-colours and small panels that I had painted with acrylics, using them as if they were oils. I had hoped to find this new medium as good as oils: the quicker drying made it very convenient for packing, and in the Arctic, where the temperature hovered around freezing, acrylics were quite satisfactory. But a year later, when I tried them for a painting trip in the Rockies in warm weather, they were a disaster, drying on the palette before I could use them and clogging the brushes. Worst of all, as they dried they changed tone, darkening and making it impossible to patch an area. However, a finished painting is indistinguishable from one in oils. I have to look at the date on the back of a panel to know whether it is painted in oil or acrylic.

In my last year at Central Tech all the art teachers under the jurisdiction of the Board of Education had been invited down to College Street for a lecture from the new principal of the Ontario College of Art. He was an inspiring speaker, visionary, revolutionary, opening vistas to me that shook me up and left me eager for more. I decided to enrol as a regular student in the college from which I had graduated more than forty years before. I made out the application, assembled the required portfolio of work, took it down for the obligatory personal interview, and was accepted. Alas, before the end of term the principal had been fired. Although long on inspiration, as an administrator he was apparently a total loss, and had already wrecked the financial situation at the college and split staff and students into factions that were tearing it apart. I was lucky to have been able to find fresh inspiration elsewhere.

But I felt ready for something. I missed the stimulus of those craft classes at CTS, and in mid-September of 1973 I decided to join Frances Dalziel in a course at the University of Toronto. Father Bellyea of St. Michael's College gave one called Religious Concepts in Literature that two of Fran's children had enjoyed and recommended. In the ten years since Frannie Bennett had lived with me, "Big Fran," her other godmother, had lost her doctor husband to cancer, sold the big family house they had shared, and become my next-door neighbour.

I then discovered that university began weeks earlier than in my youth and I was already late in applying. I would have to go in person to Woodsworth College and obtain special permission to submit a late application. To my astonishment I was refused, on the grounds that a person of my age would not be able to catch up two weeks' missed classes. I protested. I pointed out that the work I had been doing as a teacher and as an artist was demanding and complex, and expressed my confidence that I could make up the lost time. My interviewer was adamant, and there was no appeal from her decision.

Father Bellyea let me sit in at the lectures and I did the assignments for the fun of it, but without registration no credit was earned. I learned one lesson from that and registered in plenty of time for Northrop Frye's class the next year. Through the rest of the seventies and into the eighties the university was my delight, my stimulus, my tonic. I moved to Scarborough College, originally for reasons of convenience and then because I found there my own community, and a level of good teaching that impressed me very much.

In the early seventies I felt that it was time to broaden my field of exhibitions and become known beyond Toronto. Bora Laskin, newly elevated to be Chief Justice of Canada, encouraged me to think of Ottawa. I knew the Robertson Gallery by reputation, but when I wrote to John Robertson to ask if he were interested, I did not know that the Arctic was his specialty. He replied enthusiastically, and I had my first solo show there in February 1974.

It was a beautiful gallery, well hung, with none of the posters and miscellany that had cluttered the Gutenberg Gallery. I stayed with Peggy and Bora, in the luxury of a room where I could lie in bed and see the lights of all Ottawa twinkling below me. Barbara Laskin, now married to Tim Plumptre, gave the after-opening party at their home in the Glebe, and my loved ones gathered in force to support me. The Scullions were on their way back from a holiday in England and routed themselves through Ottawa. Flo came, and Marjorie and Roy from

Toronto. Stewart MacDonald and some of the other naturalists rallied. Wyn and Beryl Plumptre and Peggy and Bora were there. Old students, Bruce Garner, Peggy Graner, Philip Weiss, now all successful artists settled in Ottawa, Dalton Muir and Herbie Low of the Arctic Institute, Maurice Haycock, and some VIPs from the diplomatic world, thanks undoubtedly to Peggy's generous interest, made it a big opening and a glamorous one.

It was at that opening that Margaret Pickersgill asked me why I had never painted in Newfoundland and told me that she had a cottage there, where I could stay if I liked. Margaret was married to Jack Pickersgill, the minister in charge of fisheries in Pearson's government, the member for Twillingate and an important part of the Newfoundland scene. Margaret had been born a Beattie, a connection of Ginny's family, and was therefore prepared to accept me on trust as a good thing. I took her up on that offer. In 1975, with Madeleine Moir, Malcolm's sister, I made the first of many painting trips to our newest province and fell in love with it. Madeleine and I both painted there, but the best work of art to come out of our stay that summer was not a painting. It was Madeleine's big wooden collage of driftwood, fishing gear, and flotsam, which is a unique feature of Margaret's cottage to this day.

Another contact made at the Ottawa opening gave me a companion for my spring painting trip to Arctic Bay. Dorothy ("Dotch") Peck, small, my age, abrupt, talked to me. "I've never been to the Arctic," she said. "I'd love to go." "Do you want to come with me?" I asked. "I'm going in April, by myself, and if you want to come, do."

We exchanged addresses and, with no more previous

acquaintance than that, did travel north together and lived in another "hung basement" just vacated by the settlement manager, who had built his own home and was (more or less) moved into it. April was already past the equinox and had lovely light and quite long days, but it was winter. Everything was snow, even the tops of the hills. The world was white, very different from the Arctic Bay I had seen en route to Pond two years before. And it was cold, usually fifteen or twenty degrees below zero. I carried only oils. This was the lowest temperature I had ever tried to paint in, far colder than Haliburton at Christmas.

I would go out in the morning into bright sunshine, in loose moccasins with thick newspaper insoles over two pair of socks, wearing long underwear, my indoor slacks and a pair of thick warm-up pants over that, an extra sweater under my hooded T-shirt and over that my thick down parka, with a wool toque and a brimmed cotton sun-hat tied on with a silk kerchief. The great joy of having our own house was that we could keep the temperature at a reasonable sixty-eight degrees, but even so it was essential that before I dressed for outdoors I had already set up my sketch-box, laid the colours out on the palette, and packed my knapsack with turps, lucite medium, blow-up pillow, plenty of paint rags and a litter bag for them, and my beat-up old yellow plastic slicker in case of wind. Once I had my clothes on and had dropped a tube of white paint down my front to lodge in my bra and keep warm, I leapt out the front door so as not to steam up.

The village is built around the sloping shore of a bay. Behind it are high hills. It has three or four rows of houses, the usual pre-fabs, parallel to the shore, each one higher up the slope. Winter traffic is by snowmobile, and is busy. My problem was to keep my footing on the well-polished slope of the village. Laden as I was, every step saw me skidding downhill as far as the step took me forward. My own giggles added to the difficulty. It was a great relief to find some place against a house or dog kennel that would shelter me from the wind and let the sun reach me. I would blow up the cushion, find a piece of wood or a lump of snow thick enough to counteract the slope and make it level, lower myself on to it gingerly, spread out my legs wide enough to position the sketch-box in front of me, level it with my slicker, perhaps, stick the handles of my brushes into the snow beside me, open my box, pour out an inch or so of medium into one of the twin cups and turps into the other, pull out a panel from the slotted lid of the box, lean it against the lid as an easel, and, at last, look about me.

Before I sat down I might have seen something that suggests an idea, but this is the moment of truth. I must find some aspect of all these riches to make the point of my story, the focus of my painting. I might choose the distant hills, where the first clouds to appear are throwing delicate shadows across the pink distance and offering pattern. Or I can look instead at the hill on my left, noble King George, whose sides are so sheer that there are strips of pink rock colour showing above the snow. I might concentrate on the fantastic forms of the pressure ice and let the distant mountains be background, or by turning my head centre on two small houses and the

upturned boats between them down close to the shore. I
must decide quickly, before the cold penetrates, but tomorrow is also a day, and a chance for a different choice.
Today I settle for the pressure ice, and choose one angular
cluster of ice shapes to dominate the composition.

With thin colour, turps with just a hint of blue in it, I
make three quick lines, enough to place the mass off
centre, low enough to leave room for the far hills, high
enough to allow some less eccentric snow shapes to take
the eye upwards and inwards to the centre of interest.
With bold light lines I establish the shore-line and the
swinging movement of the distant mountains, and plot
two or three shapes of foreground snow forms. It is
important that the lines look confident. I may change
them later, but shaky uncertain lines are death to a sketch.
I am using arm and wrist movements, holding my long-
handled brush by the end, still in gloves. Then I sit back
and evaluate. Unless the shapes are already well balanced, rhythmic in their relationships, interesting, I
should not go on with it. From the very first strokes the
painting must have enough life to give some of its energy
back to me, sustaining me through the whole process of
development.

Next I begin to work out the tone scheme, establishing
the dark areas and seeing how well the pattern of dark
and light tells the story. For this I still use a turps wash,
not yet worrying about subtleties of colour. Sometimes I
roll sideways at this point, swinging my leg across my
sketch-box and getting to my feet to back away and judge
the composition from farther off. This is my last chance
to revise it. Once back on my cushion I am doing final
work. I fish out my warm white paint and squeeze some

on to my palette. Usually I start with the most challenging and complex forms, probably my centre of interest, looking for the colour in the light and in the cast shadows, and the much more complex colour that is reflected into the side of the form that is turned away from the light. Every brushstroke must describe the form by its direction and texture as well as by its tone and colour. I am always drawing in paint. Most often I start my painting in the sky and work down towards the foreground for the sake of having the near forms lie on top of those farther off.

In less time than it has taken to describe the process I have chilled off and need a "bush" badly. I can stop now because all the critical bits are fully painted or I have at least established the exact colour and tone. Perhaps it is the buzz of the snowmobiles with the stepped-up traffic of noon-hour that has reminded me that the morning has gone and it's time to struggle home again. Getting back is even more difficult than coming. My hands, even in gloves, are so stiff that I can hardly open the bottles to pour back the lucite and turps that I have not used. Both are far too precious to waste. I wipe the brushes and put them in the box facing in the wrong direction so that I will know which ones need washing. Used paint-rags are gathered into my litter bag. (Forty years ago Peter Haworth gave me an unforgettable bawling-out for leaving an empty paint-tube on location. Even in the Arctic, which sometimes looks to me like one great garbage dump, I cannot forget that lesson.) I slide the painting into its slot, wet side away from me, and close the box. Once again I roll sideways over it and get painfully up on my stiff legs, frozen into position after so long apart, squeeze the air out of my cushion, and pack it with slicker,

litter bag, camera, and whatever else I have brought into
the knapsack. It goes over one shoulder, the box over the
other, with a strap collar joining them and keeping them
from falling down my arms, and I am ready for the sliding
and slipping back, uphill this time, to sanctuary.

Dotch was a good companion on that trip. Like Roberta
before her, she found her greatest pleasure in the children
of the village, and played endless games of tag with the
pre-schoolers around the hummocks of sea ice. Besides
the many Inuit friends she made, there were two young
couples, whites, the Stilwells and the Loneys, all four of
them teachers, who entertained us in their homes, took a
lively interest in my work, and made sure that we saw
more than the village, taking us off up over the back hill
by snowmobile, and on a cook-out meal some miles away
around the far headland, and encouraging us to join in
the fun that came with the Arctic Games.

This was an annual festival to which the Inuit from
other settlements and as far away as Greenland came. For
a week the population of Arctic Bay doubled. We went
to one of the indoor evenings in the community hall,
where everybody gathered, from the infants in their
mothers' hoods to the really aged matriarchs, for throat
singing, arm wrestling, leg wrestling, and all the other
games that can be played indoors. In the daytime, out on
the sea beyond the rough pressure ice, there were races
for children, for adults, and for snowmobiles, tugs of war,
contests where the long dog-whips were used to flick one
small tin off another, and a great deal of standing around
talking and laughing. The Greenland Inuit were conspic-

uous in their bulky polar-bearskin pants. In Canada the
Inuit are allowed to sell that fur, and it fetches such a high
price that it would be too extravagant to wear it.

My favourite of all the games was the igloo-building
race. Tents are better than igloos as permanent or semi-
permanent homes because the oil lamps used to heat an
igloo and make it more comfortable melt the inside surface, glazing it and eventually destroying the marvellous
insulating properties of the dry snow. But for temporary
shelter while travelling, igloos are matchless. The game
started on a stretch of clean snow, and each contestant
marked out a round site and began to cut big blocks from
the snow, arranging the blocks to form a circular wall.
The secret of success is choosing snow that is dry and
dense enough to make firm building-blocks. The first
block must be made wedge-shaped, from nothing at the
low end to a foot or more high at the other. The base is
cut so that the block leans slightly in, and the high end
carved back at an angle to allow the next block to lean
against it without falling forward. Each successive block
carries the wall a bit higher so that the igloo grows in a
spiral, diminishing in radius as it rises. The builder works
from inside, deepening the floor as he cuts and shapes
more blocks. He uses a long, broad knife specially designed for the purpose. He may have to leave the igloo to
complete it with a further supply of snow blocks. Certainly he must leave it to drop the final block over the
opening at the top. He cuts a door in the bottom row and
a smoke hole at the top, and the igloo is complete for
contest purposes. Fifteen minutes was the winner's time.

The next day the young Stilwells, Mike and Irene, took
me off out of sight of the village to build our own. This

was no fifteen-minute job. It took us a long afternoon, but we added some refinements. While Mike cut and shaped the blocks, Rene and I caulked the cracks with soft snow and smoothed the surface. After the doorway was cut, Mike made a storm porch, a tunnel two or three feet deep leading to the door, one extra big block on each side and another to make a roof for it. Inside we had left a sleeping platform opposite the door, a foot or so higher than the floor. Mike knew that these were essential features of a real igloo, and he and Rene intended to sleep in this one. I bitterly regretted having to leave Arctic Bay too soon to join them. The most favourite picture I have ever had taken is of the front of our igloo, with Doris's head and shoulders emerging from the storm porch and a look of smug bliss spread all over my Irish face. The scarf that covers my chin is a reminder that it had been frozen on our skidoo trip a couple of days before and was black and blue and still in sad need of protection.

While I was in Arctic Bay, I found in the Co-op shop a magnificent whalebone carving of a hunter thrusting a harpoon at a narwhal. It is carved from the biggest single piece of whalebone I have ever seen, an epic sculpture. The sculptor lived in the village, a young Inuit, shy but pleased that I had bought his work. When it had been shipped home, I put it outside the big living-room window. It was wonderful there, but by the end of the summer I realized that, being bone, it was vulnerable to attack from insects and even from birds. It came indoors to a less dramatic setting, where it is still my joy and a constant reminder of Arctic Bay.

6

Everything Which Is Yes

MY DIARY FOR THE SPRING of 1974 is full of details about sales of paintings, fresh delight in the garden, and the new-found pleasures of retirement. In the early days of teaching I had discovered that branches of mountain ash in their September glory of red berries were good for beginners either to draw or to paint, and for several years I brought a supply of mountain ash in with me at the beginning of term. After a few years of this, the berries turning red in the fall made me feel sick with their message of the prison doors looming. I began to hate the sight of mountain ash. When retirement was imminent, I bought a young tree and planted it near the patio, where every September it would remind me that I was on permanent reprieve. The first morning of a visit to Fool's Paradise by Dotch Peck, we woke to find that a racoon had climbed the slender little tree and broken its trunk right in half. It looked hopeless to me, but not to Dotch.

"You can put it together again with splints and a bandage," she assured me. Dotch held the top in position while I coaxed the torn ends together, caulked the joint with asphaltum, bound it with cloth over splints, and drove in a strong stake beside it, guyed to hold it steady. Finally we tied the ash to the stake and crossed our fingers. Today the lovely tall tree, with a slight bump in its trunk, is a living memorial to Dotch, and a constant reminder to me to rejoice in my freedom.

It was after Dotch had left, one Monday morning in late May, when I was down in the front field raking hay and remembering my retirement year when I had raked hay and wondered if my thyroid operation would discover cancer, that I heard the phone ring up at the house. I ran for it and caught it before it stopped ringing.

Roy's voice was desperate. "Doris, come quickly. Marjorie's terribly sick." I grabbed my purse and jumped in the car, allowing myself to feel nothing but hurry – hurry. She was in bed, still warm in my arms, but already dead. She and Roy had spent Sunday with Mar and Tom and the children in Hamilton and come home in the evening. In the morning after breakfast Marjorie had felt a little unwell and gone back to bed to sleep it off. This pattern of tiredness, nausea, and headache was very old, familiar since school-days, when I used to help her home on a Friday afternoon after a week of too much excitement.

Roy had gone up just before noon to see if she was ready for some lunch and called me when he couldn't rouse her. The doctor confirmed that she had died in her sleep.

My normal response to emergency is to stop feeling. I can act in whatever way seems to meet the situation, but I go numb inside. I stayed with Roy through the next few hours, organizing the phone calls that he was incapable of thinking about, admitting the coroner and the undertakers when they came, making tea for the family members who began to gather. Anne, Marjorie's eldest, was in Australia, and there were cables to send and overseas phone calls to arrange. By the time I was no longer needed for practical help, I had remembered the dinner-party that was due at my house that evening.

It was a small party, just Nancy, with Hugh Stiff and Brian Freeland, the two men who twenty years before had been young priests keeping St. Aidan's going after Dr. English became ill. I decided not to tell them about Marjorie. The shell of me that was left could produce the food and drinks, keep the fire bright, and let the old friends enjoy being together again after the years that Hugh had spent out west becoming a bishop. I did tell Nan so that she would cover for me when needed. It was no worse for me to be serving a dinner and listening to the men talk than it would have been to be alone or with anyone else. Only Marjorie could have shared this, as she had shared everything else of great importance in my life, and she was no longer here to share it. I knew that this night was the beginning of the rest of my life. Nothing would ever be the same again, and I would have to get used to it.

I can find no words adequate to say what Marjorie meant in my life. Our friendship taught me how to love. All the wrong ways were ready to trip me up in my teens after she had met her new friends at camp and university.

Her steadiness towards me dissolved my jealousy as I discovered that new love did not cast out old, that hearts grow larger to allow an endless growth in the capacity to love. This I had already learned before she married. After that my life was widening while hers was deepening, but space never separated us. Always she was with me, part of the very fabric of my being. Our friendship became the norm of other friendships, so that I offered to Ginny and Nan and Flo and expected from them the same acceptance, trust, and loyalty. This was what friendship meant.

Even in the first realization of having lost her, I could not be sorry for myself. I had known Marjorie, had lived with her for fifty-six years, loved by her, loving her, sharing tears and laughter, rich beyond deserving. My prayer was thanksgiving. In all the years of our friendship, to think of her was to rejoice, and it still was.

The summer after Marjorie's death Roy came up to Georgian Bay for a few days. He showed me where he had buried Marjorie's ashes up on Ben Hole, the bald granite hill back of the cottages. It had a shallow depression on its crown. While Roy was there we trundled barrow-full after barrow-full of rich composted earth up the hill to deepen the soil in the hollow where her ashes lay. We found three young pines and brought them, roots and all, to plant there. Then Roy hauled a hundred pails of water up the hill to saturate the soil and give the young trees a good start. Today there are three beautiful white pines crowning the hill, surviving wind, drought, winter storms. Perhaps I shall even see the day when they are tall enough to be landmarks from a distance, like Spyglass at Silver Island.

Roy showed me a poem Marjorie had written not long before she died.

PETITION

Let me drop into a pool of silence
Where no words fall.
Let me lie in ambient light
Within dark privacy.
Let no least breath of blossom
Sweeten my air,
No rough taste of bread or drink
Unsober my mouth.
And oh! Let no touch of flesh on flesh
People me.
Yet – lest I drown – keep underneath
Love's arms of everlasting

(In full times I shall deliver me
Out of this second womb –
And a stiller life begin.)

Marjorie and Roy were members of Metropolitan United Church in downtown Toronto, where she had been at the heart of the group that introduced dance and drama into the Sunday services. This experiment had grown into Dayspring, a weekend festival of all the arts held every May. Marjorie's friends at the church wanted to do something special as a memorial to her. It had to be art. It had to say something about Marjorie's genius for people, for

loving them and for working happily with them. It had to
be fun. They talked it over with Roy and me. I went down
to the church by myself to let the building speak to me,
and sitting at the back, looking towards the Gothic arch
that frames the chancel, I could see that the blank white
spaces on either side of the arch were crying out for
colour. I began to visualize a magnificent banner hanging
down either side. Thinking about it, I realized that it
would be possible to involve everyone who had known
Marjorie by letting each of them share in the actual work
of making the banners.

Cliff Elliott, the minister, invited all those interested to
come to the parish hall one Saturday morning in the
autumn of 1974 for a day-long work session. I was there
with a supply of paper – white, black, and brown, saucers
of flour paste, and all the scissors we could borrow from
the Sunday school. The Dayspring people were on hand,
ready to help. Roy and a young doctor-husband were the
first men to volunteer, although Cliff and his assistant
were hovering about to give us moral support. Their
wives joined us. Marjorie's eldest daughter, Anne,
brought her two children, not to play around but to get
in there with both hands. Marg Cork turned up, arthritis
and all, along with two other of Marjorie's classmates
from Victoria College, class of '31. We four had all been
to CGIT camp together back in the twenties, and Mary,
who came down from Rosedale, had been one of our
camp leaders before she married Henry Jackman. Another Mary, half her age, from the subsidized housing at
Regent Park, brought a friend who had sewing skills that
she thought we could use. We were a mixed bag of more
than thirty men, women, and children.

I gathered them together and explained the general plan: one banner to tell the story of the life of Jesus, the other to show the Holy Spirit as we had seen it in Marjorie's life. Each of them was asked to make a picture for each banner out of cut paper. By limiting them to black, white, and half-tone, I assured myself that no one would bog down in subtleties that would be lost at a distance.

There were a few slow starters, afraid of their own lack of experience. But scissors free the hands (shades of my first days of teaching); images appeared. I went around encouraging, showing how to enlarge and simplify, delighted by the original ideas emerging. Seven-year-old Paul decided to make Grandma's garden and to put in it the rabbit and the skunk he had once seen there. His nine-year-old sister thought that Marjorie's kitchen had been full of the Holy Spirit, and there is the kitchen today, half-way up the right-hand banner, with a white electric stove on a green background, with loaves of bread fresh from the oven and shelves along the top stocked with pots and pans. One patch showed a field of wheat. Another had a large windmill behind a line of blowing clothes, recalling Marjorie's love of wind and wind poetry.

The banner of the life of Christ was more predictable, thanks, I suppose, to everyone's having been brought up with stained-glass windows and reproductions of old masters. Fortunately, these are impossible to copy in appliqué. So facial expressions were replaced with gesture and body language, and symbols were found for ideas that were too difficult for literal representation.

By the middle of the afternoon, when we were all tired, almost everyone had arrived at some idea worth develop-

ing. I sent them home to search for fabrics and to come
back the next week with whatever they could round up
that might be useful, while I carried off their designs to
look them over and make them workable. After that we
met on week-night evenings, in groups small enough for
individual attention. They made tracings of each part of
their pictures and cut them out in fabric, leaving extra so
that the edges could be turned under and pressed flat to
avoid fraying. We tested the composition by walking
away from it the length of the corridor. If we could still
read it clearly and understand its story, it was ready for
stitching. By midwinter thirty-one panels were brought
back finished.

Each of the panels was a rectangle, but they were of
every colour and size, some vertical, some horizontal, and
I had wide white sheeting for the background. I began at
the bottom on that first banner with the Incarnation, and
on up to the dramatic events of the Passion. There were
gaps and some quite large blank areas, but I was able to
lead the eye from panel to panel by using texts. I played
around with the shapes, up and down the step-ladder,
pinning and unpinning. Tones must balance, and there
must be a reasonable distribution of the bright reds and
strong darks, leading up to the Resurrection scenes at the
top as the climax.

To unify the banner of the Holy Spirit I used the poem
by e.e. cummings that Marjorie had hung in her front hall.

> i thank You God for most this amazing
> day: for the leaping greenly spirits of trees
> and a blue true dream of sky; and for everything
> which is natural which is infinite which is yes

The triumphant affirmation in those lines was right for her. She embraced life. And the poem allowed me to carry the eye up from the "I thank you God" across the bottom to an enormous flaming scarlet "YES" at the top.

"February 28, 1975: Marjorie came to me Monday night. There is no other word for the experience, although it happened in the sleep-dream-five-o'clock-in-the-morning hour after a wakeful first of the night. I was in her kitchen with Roy, and in answer to someone's saying, 'It's terrible not being able to talk it over with her,' there she was, perched on the edge of the table. 'We can still talk it over together,' and she held out her arms to me and I held her tight and was held, and I hid my face in her so that I wouldn't need to speak, and then I turned to Roy to ask if he could see her too. Absolutely vivid and convincing, and when I woke or whatever, I wept as I have not wept before. I have shed very few tears for my darling, but being with her again dissolved all my steely controls."

Once more I gathered the faithful on a Saturday morning. The church gymnasium had a balcony high enough up so that with two tall women standing on chairs on the balcony and holding the fabric as high as they could reach, the banner could hang to the floor of the gym and let us see the whole thing at once from a distance. The workers took turns so that everyone had a chance to see and approve. Then we laid the fabric out on long trellis tables and all worked at stitching the panels into position. When we left that day, only hemming and inspection remained to be done.

Except for the hanging – except for the hanging. The ceiling retreated into heaven. No ladder could reach it, and Roy and I had to find some way of raising the banners into position and lowering them again. Up the hundred or so steps of the spiral staircase in the tower at the front of the church we climbed, with all the tools we thought we might need. In the gloom of the attic we found a narrow catwalk running the length of the nave. Roy crept out on a rafter to reach the right spots and bored holes for the wire hangers. He fed the wires down through the holes and put them over pulleys up in the attic. I was down below chasing the ends, fastening them to the rods, and directing the levelling.

The afternoon was spent, and the daylight fading. Roy spiralled back down to join me, found the right switch, and flooded the church with light. Then the great moment came when we two stood together at the back of the nave, and saw that it was good. And wished Marjorie had been there to share our pleasure.

About ten years later I had my only other dream of her. It was at the cottage. I was in the studio, at work in front of my easel, when I heard her call, the familiar ki-oh-ki that was our private signal. I knew that she was dead and that I must be mistaken, but I rushed out and there just outside the door she stood, smiling. My first reaction was to notice how well she looked, younger than when she died. "It's all right," she said. "It's nothing to be afraid of." I knew that she was talking about my death, and that I could believe her. I stood with her for a while, comfortable as I was only with her.

What does my dream of Marjorie mean to me? A precious experience of once more being with her. I have no theories about any afterlife. I cannot imagine that the old concepts of heaven are true. Yet I ask myself, who could possibly have imagined life as we have found it?

2nd dream of Marjorie

God - our image of goodness

When I do think about what comes after death, and of course as I get older death is oftener in my mind, I always conclude that it is none of my business. My concern is with here and now, how to live every day to the full, in love. If there is more to come, good. If not, I have not wasted what I was given. I respond to the poetry of the book of Revelation with its vision of the City of God, the New Jerusalem, and to all the other stirring words that poets have written in affirmation of that vision. I share the universal yearning for love, goodness, and peace that finds expression in the imagery of the kingdom of God on earth and in heaven. I am glad of the music, the sculpture, and the painting that celebrate man's hunger for a better world than this. It is what makes us human, this image of goodness that many of us call God. This is the thing that separates us from the other animals.

Today I find it all too easy to believe that the world may come to a cataclysmic end, but I do not blame God for that nor expect any miraculous sorting of the sheep and the goats after death. We are sorting ourselves every day as we make the choices that we must make within the little freedom given to us by our genes and the world we are born into.

"So how can an intelligent woman like you go to church?" one of my neighbours asked me a few years ago. I was reminded of my early teens, when we were confronted with the conflict between the scientists' discoveries of evolution and the authority of the Bible. Dr. Cotton, the rector at St. Aidan's who prepared me for confirmation, assured me then that God intended us to use our brains and that the evidence of fossils and living nature was to be trusted.

But the question challenges and teases me. Sometimes I suspect that I go to church because Nan Wright's breakfast parties are too good to miss. The oval table is set with six places, always flowers and candles, always her home-made bread or Jan's muffins or both, always a bowl of fruit salad, always the best tea of the week and many cups of it, always good talk and laughter. But the quality of those parties depends on the unspoken commitments we share. So what are they?

As I grew, read, studied, and thought, I learned very well that Jesus might be goodness incarnate, another way of saying God, but that Christianity and the Church were not all good. The denominations and sects that make up the Church are just people, and however dedicated, however sincere, they are human, full of all the folly, blindness, mixed motives, self-deceit, vanity, sloth – what are the seven deadly sins? Name them and we've got them. So why belong to an organization that I see as so imperfect?

Because it keeps before my eyes the perfection that it misses so tragically. Because it reminds me of eternity, and my values get a salutary shake-up that distances me from my petty triumphs and petty miseries. It's true that sometimes the whole service washes over me and leaves me dry. It is true also that I can be so irritated by technical faults in the liturgy, even by mispronunciation, that I miss the nourishment that is being offered. But I do believe in the validity of what we are trying to do. And I do realize that to do it better, St. Aidan's needs bodies in the pews,

money on the plate, and people to smile at their neighbours and greet them by name.

This is a long way from the ecstatic mood of the
torchlight ceremonies at CGIT camp, where I first was
seized by the vision. But the Transfiguration that we read
about in the Gospels wasn't permanent either, only a brief
moment of insight. Even in the humdrum of daily life, love
makes the sun shine, and love lives in the small acts of
kindness and caring that even quite ordinary people can
be inspired to do.

On Christmas Eve, at the big midnight service, I watch
the long line of worshippers coming down from the Com-
munion railing after kneeling there to receive the bread
and the wine. Most of them I know from having worked
with them over the years in the Nativity play. The children who were cherubs around the crib then are getting
old enough to be angels now. The boys that I used as
shepherds could be Roman soldiers today. Mary, now
mother of three, no longer looks virginal. Herod has put
on weight. All ages, sizes, and shapes of them are here to
join in the ritual, the "outward and visible sign of an
inward and spiritual grace," as the old catechism put it.
They are my family.

The temperature of my spiritual life varies from day to
day and year to year. There are high times, like the
wonderful farewell party for Don Purser before he left to
go and live with his grand-daughter in Ottawa. That night
there was a surge of warmth and love that seemed to unite
us all. Not long after, there was a vestry meeting with
tensions so tangible that I felt that the Church might fly
apart.

But without the Church, how are today's children to hear that there are better goals than those pressed on them by television commercials? How are we to find common expression of the vision of goodness that makes us human? What other hands are offered to clasp in the dark? I see the Church as the necessary human organization to keep alive the knowledge of Jesus, who understood better than anyone else before or since what is true goodness, who taught that this was what God was, and who lived out in his life and death the vision he had seen. Through the centuries, theologians, artists, musicians, and poets have added their tributes, and sometimes their distortions, to our knowledge and understanding of Jesus, clothing him in the mythology of Christianity. We can embrace these glories and enjoy them as long as we don't let them hide what they were intended to celebrate. I don't believe that Anglicanism or any other form of Christianity is the only road to God. Nory needed the teachings of the Baha'i religion to help her find the meaning of life and a fellowship to share it. God is as real to my Jewish friends as to me, and when I was travelling in the East I found myself recognizing his presence in the mosques.

Love in my family and then with Marjorie was the experience that opened me to spiritual values. Christianity is the context in which I first met Him-Her-Them, in the church, at CGIT camp, in the Student Christian Movement, and therefore it is appropriate as my community of faith.

Marjorie's banners were the beginning for me of a series of liturgical wall-hangings. The first was for a side chapel at St. Aidan's, a memorial to Dr. English, and shows the Doc himself, big nose and stocky figure, in a black cassock, surrounded by the junior girls' choir, the boys of the servers' guild, and the costumed figures of the Nativity play, all his innovations, as well as a capsule history of the saint and of the parish named for him. It is colourful, and fun.

My favourite of all the liturgical hangings I have made is the one at Cana Place, a new residence in Scarborough for the elderly run by the Anglican Sisters of St. John the Divine. The Sisters invited me to look at a bare room and suggest how it could become a chapel.

Cana was a village in Galilee where Jesus is reported by St. John to have attended a wedding and to have changed the water into wine. The story is charming, full of very human concerns familiar to anyone who has been responsible for making a party go. As a metaphor for the transformation of life experienced by a Christian, water into wine is apt, and the words of the wine steward, "You have kept the good wine until now," appealed to me as a beautiful analogy of the experience of growing old happily. For a text to dominate the hanging I chose Mary's words to her agitated hostess: "Whatever he tells you to do, do it."

I had a big area to cover with the story, permitting the important figures to be about three feet high, with features on their faces and a fair amount of detail. Appliqué is a coarse medium. However carefully you cut a mouth two inches wide, the turning under of the edges and the stitching can produce unexpected results. You may need to try again. In the case of Mary, whom I had represented as a mature woman, she ended up looking faintly amused.

I was delighted, and realized for the first time that when Jesus and his brothers and sisters were young, their home must have been full of laughter.

I wondered if the whole mood of the hanging was too light-hearted, so I asked the Sisters to come down to my studio to see it pinned together before I started the stitching. They loved it, and we made sure that the elderly residents would accept it by allowing each of them to do a token amount of the sewing. For the carpet and the chair cushions in the chapel the sisters chose the same cherry red I had used freely in the hanging. The room sings.

While Nan was still Nancy Caudle she had shared painting trips, Stratford, and St. Aidan's with me. Since her husband, Ken Wright, died, after only seven years of marriage, and her ninety-five-year-old mother shortly afterwards, Nan has been my painting companion, my ally. Her commitment to the life of the spirit is complete, but not to the exclusion of a zest for the whole of the rest of life. Her arms are open, and her doors. St. Aidan's Church is full of Nancy's art and of mine. One of the original "magnificent banners" found its devious way to the narthex, high over one of the doors. Nan's processional banners appear on every high day. My crêche figures are a big feature of Christmas and Epiphany. The war-memorial book is my work, although the binding of it was done by Madeline of my CGIT group. Nan stole the rock from the ancient ruin at Lindisfarne, where Aidan founded his abbey in the sixth century, while I stood look-out. I designed and made the mosaic setting for it, and wrote the screed explaining its connection with Saint Aidan. Nan arranged and framed the purple stole that was worn by our first rector and did the lettering on the plaque in the chapel. I lettered and gilded the inscription in the baptistry that was built at the back of the church in memory of Doctor Cotton. Nan designed and decorated the memorial bookstand on the pulpit. The chapel wall-hanging is mine. Nan helped me to mount the door panels that our current rector asked me to create to offer a more colourful welcome to the church than the shabby old brown baize that they cover.

We wince together over some of the visual decisions that were made without us, and there were many. But neither of us imagines that the building, with its beauties or its uglinesses, is what the Church is all about. We know that it is about the holy spirit that filled Marjorie and spilled over to all who knew her, about love, which was St. John's definition of God, and the best one I have found in my long life.

7

Widening Horizons

THE SEVENTIES WERE YEARS of great change in my life. Marjorie's death in 1974 was the most devastating. The summer after that, while I was in England with Nan, Ginty died quite suddenly, and I came home to Milly bereft, and the pattern of eleven years gone forever. Milly went to live with another old friend who had a home in north Toronto, and I began a regime of short-term cat-sitters.

There were some good changes as well. My professional life was expanding. Not only was I showing in Ottawa every other year, but I had made contact with the Kensington Gallery in Calgary and was having regular exhibitions in the city of my birth. Usually I was able to combine travel to a Calgary opening with a painting trip in the mountains.

About this time Jack Firestone of Ottawa bought a number of sketches, canvases, and water-colours. He had been collecting Canadian art for some time and was in the process of deeding his home and collection to the city of Ottawa to establish it as a permanent gallery. Among his acquisitions were a great many works by the Group of Seven. He asked me for an example of what I had done in each year since I had begun to paint. He had already assembled a similar record of the work of A.J. Casson, and I was flattered to be included in such distinguished company. Since it was understood to be a public collection, with some paintings and sketches always hanging on view and the others available for research at any time, I sent off to Ottawa many of my favourite works.

Free at last to travel when and where I would, I made periodic trips to Newfoundland and to the Rockies, and followed the Scullions and other northern friends about in the High Arctic.

Mike Stilwell had become the settlement manager at Grise Fiord, and I was invited there in 1976. The most northerly of all the Arctic villages, Grise was established to maintain Canadian sovereignty. Inuit families from Baker Lake in northern Quebec and others from Pond Inlet were settled in an area of good hunting on the south shore of Ellesmere Island, on a long beach under towering cliffs of rock. To fly in to Grise in summer, as I did with the naturalists in 1972, the aircraft aims straight at these cliffs, and just before striking them and dashing itself to pieces, it swerves sharp left and circles down to a small level patch on top of a hill nestled among the mountains. Everyone hurries up the hill by truck or on foot, perhaps to celebrate the miracle, or just to see who has come.

Grise in April was in deep winter, even colder than

Arctic Bay, but a landing-strip had been marked out down on the sea ice, and our arrival was a little less hair-raising this time. As we flew in we passed over half a dozen captive icebergs scattered out in the bay in front of the village.

To me as a painter, these were riches, and to the community riches for a different reason. Grise depended on these bergs for its water supply. All day long water-men on snowmobiles roared back and forth collecting ice. From morning till late afternoon we heard the strokes of the axes as they hacked away at the berg, and we watched them drag back the sleds with boxes of ice. They went from house to house, leaving a couple of chunks in the wooden crib outside each one. When the water inside the Stilwell house was getting low, Mike carried in an arm-load of ice and dumped it into the cistern to melt at its leisure.

"April 12: I'm a dead duck, having walked out to the icebergs and around them taking photographs, and back again, two hours' steady slugging, and my right hand frozen in the process, or so it felt. All I really suffered was pain when the feeling came back. The bergs are wonder-ful. One has an eighteen-inch-wide band of brilliant blue ice, cobalt, running vertically the whole height of the berg. Others were green, pure nile, and the snow that has fallen on them made white patterns that I have not seen before."

Out beyond the last berg there was an ice-research camp, a colourful cluster of red igloo-shaped tents. Mike flew me out in a helicopter and stayed long enough for me to make a sketch. Inside the tent where I eventually retreated to thaw out there was an impressive bank of sophisticated electronic equipment ticking away as it registered sea-bottom temperatures. We were offered tea hospitably but warned that the rolls of LifeSaver candies on the ledge of the computer case were for business, not pleasure. It was amusing to hear that some high-tech underwater procedure had failed until one of the boys discovered how to make it work by installing a LifeSaver, which would melt after a suitable interval and release a cord to position a small gauge where it was meant to be.

The research station had another entertaining home-made device. Surrounding the camp was a wide circle of wire held up from the ice by posts and strung at intervals with empty tin cans, a polar-bear alarm. If a foraging bear should wander towards the camp, the researchers would have a chance to gain time by throwing it handfuls of dog-burgers to distract it until they could take more drastic defensive action. I never did find out what that would be. Shooting polar bears is a no-no.

Television had not yet reached the Arctic, but Grise received a regular supply of motion pictures, which were shown in the community hall in the evening. Usually I was happy to baby-sit and let Irene and Mike out, but one night I joined them. The picture was an adventure mystery with comedy overtones, but the last reel was missing. Nobody but me seemed put out when the film ended without finishing. I went back to baby-sitting.

One night after we were all in bed, the phone rang. It was someone asking Irene to get out her binoculars to see who was approaching in the distance, skidoos or dogs? It was both, first skidoos, with the RCMP men who had been off on polar-bear patrol, then three Finns who had been skiing over from Greenland, and then, farther away, two strange dog-teams, all making for the village. Since he was settlement manager, this was Mike's business. He and Irene both dressed and went down to the shore to meet the procession. From the big front window I watched the stream of villagers who ran down and out on to the ice to be there when it arrived, the skidoos whizzing out to meet the dog-sleds, the excitement, the beautiful sight of those teams of thirteen dogs, each pulling with a will, and then when they had reached the village, chaos and confusion, a jumble of dogs, sleds, children, and everyone else in the settlement.

Eventually Irene and Mike and a tall young English couple, who had come across with the dogs and their Greenland native drivers, came in, peeled off the furry parkas, the overpants, and the big boots, and settled down to a long night of talk, coffee, drinks, and a shuffling of beds that gave the visitors the bunks in my room and let me retreat to the studio downstairs (we were in another hung basement). Derek and Jenny Nordham had met such wicked ice conditions on the crossing from Greenland, so many days of blizzard too fierce for travel, that they were a week behind schedule. Instead of returning by the ice as they had intended, they would have to fly back after their visit to Grise.

Which is how I made my unexpected trip to Greenland. The Nordhams had to charter a plane to take their drivers, their dog-teams, and themselves. There was room for another person, and Mike arranged that I should be the one to make the round trip. I spent the morning down on the edge of the ice watching the loading of the plane. It took a dozen men. First the long heavy sleds, with all the gear lashed on, were eased up and into the cargo door. Then the dogs, one after another, were flung in and, like the sleds, tied into position. A flight attendant, with a pail in one hand, a shovel in the other, and a look of profound gloom on his face, stood at the door watching the drivers handle the dogs. The huskies had never been inside any building before, let alone in an aircraft, but they accepted being picked up by one driver and thrown up to the other without protest. After lunch the passengers, all five of us, were boosted up into the gaping mouth of the plane and picked our ways over dogs, between dogs, to the six seats that were clamped to the floor at the front. I sat beside the flight attendant. The driver who was sitting behind me spent the whole trip stroking a bitch who rested her head on his knee. The dogs were very funny. One would raise his voice in a sharp yelp and the plaint would be taken up by another and then another, until we were deafened by the chorus. As it was dying away, there would be a shrill note starting up again, and the crescendo would begin once more. But the pail and shovel were not needed, and the gloom on the attendant's face unjustified.

Our flight in to Greenland took us over a bay choked with captured icebergs, more than I had ever seen before or imagined. The village itself was rather forbidding, with one-storey row-housing in straight lines, painted in heavy reds, browns, and dark greens. Our pastel-coloured villages were positively lyrical by comparison. It was a brief visit, no more than a turn-around, with a quiet flight home minus dogs and their music.

Because of Grise Fiord I boast about having had

Canada's farthest-north exhibitions of art, and could
probably claim a record for proportion of the population
to have attended one.

John Scullion's last major move before he was pulled
permanently back to Ottawa was to Fort McMurray in
northern Alberta. This was when the sudden jump in the
world price of oil had made the tar sands in the area well
worth exploiting. Fort McMurray was suddenly a thriv-
ing town, and Syncrude, the company that was at the
heart of the development there, borrowed John from the
federal government to advise them about keeping their
employees happy in the isolated northern environment.
His experience working with the Inuit and other native
peoples in the Arctic was valuable to them. John considered that nowhere, and especially not at Fort McMurray,
could man live by bread alone, and one of the ways in
which he introduced a cultural dimension into the life of
the town was to bring artists of every discipline to visit
and work there.

Barbara Greene and I were invited to come and paint.
But I was already planning a trip with Nan, so she was
added to the invitation, and the three of us spent April
living with the Scullions and sketching along the Athabaska River as it flowed through the town.

Best of all were the days we spent in the Syncrude
works on the tar sands about eight miles from town. This
required security clearance and permits organized by
John, who also arranged for us to be taken there and back
in the company bus. Once at the site we were checked in
and provided with hard hats. Bar loves machinery and

industrial buildings; she was in her element. Nan and I
looked about with some dismay at pipes, chimneys,
trucks, and earth-movers of a size I had never even
imagined before. Eventually, though, we found tremen-
dous interest and excitement in painting the equipment
used for different stages of the work.

One of my happiest sessions there was spent beside the
tailings ponds. These were huge square ponds separated
by earth dikes wide enough to drive along, and therefore
wide enough for me to set up my easel and chair. The
water in these ponds was too polluted to be good for the
ducks and geese that were attracted to them. To keep the
birds away, Syncrude had set up scarecrows dressed in
vivid yellow oilskin pants and slickers, with bright red
hard hats. They were placed irregularly around the dikes,
and to reinforce their effect, beside each one was a gun
or something that sounded like one. These were com-
puter-programmed in some way to go off at random
intervals, so that the birds could not learn the pattern and
get used to it. The buildings of the processing plant and
their cluster of tall chimneys were reflected in the ponds,
with the plumes of white smoke playing against the clouds
in the blue sky. The scarecrows were comic colourful
accents in the foreground, and I provided another touch
of comedy by jumping every time one of the guns went
off.

Even more than the tailing ponds I liked the enormous
purple-black and dark brown trenches, as deep as a
skyscraper, where the huge long-necked back-hoes were
scooping out the oily sands and swinging each bucketload
up to a truck that climbed out of the canyon to haul its
load to a conveyor belt that carried it back to the plant.

It was like painting mountains in reverse. One of the buckets was lying on the ground up on top, where I could get close to it. The man working beside it who went into my sketch was a third its height.

Since Syncrude had provided us with air fare to Fort McMurray, we wanted some way of showing our appreciation and said thank you by holding a weekend workshop for all the amateur artists in town. About twenty turned out for theory sessions in the high school, painting out of doors in the heritage park close by, and a final group criticism back in the studio. Good fun, too.

The three of us finished our stay there with a well-publicized exhibition. What we didn't anticipate was that the afternoon of the opening would coincide with the going-out of the river. Winter in the north is long and tiresome. Spring is considered to have arrived the moment the ice breaks and the river is free at last. A barrel is set on the ice just below the main bridge over the Athabaska and attached by a rope to the railing. When the barrel is carried away, spring has come.

Everyone in Fort McMurray has money in some pool and has bet at what minute of what hour on what day this event will take place. Nothing can compete with this in interest. The ice had been getting shaky the day before, breaking up along the edge in places. By the morning of the day of our show, the banks of the river were spotted with people, with more arriving every minute. Eventually every man, woman, child, and dog in Fort McMurray was in the crowd. So were we three. One dog fell off an ice floe, and we held our breath too as he was carried downstream in the swirling current and rescued by a man with more courage than discretion, who ventured out on a jam and grabbed the scruff of his neck as he was struggling by.

We were lucky that the barrel went plunging in to the river before dark, and many of the townspeople did straggle in to see the paintings on their way home.

After my second Gutenberg Gallery exhibition, I began to covet a gallery that was not also a shop. Carl Gutenberg was unwilling to clear his decks of posters and other merchandise that I felt to be distracting. At that time Jack Pollock, who had been for many years on Markham Street, had acquired a beautiful space across the road from the Art Gallery of Ontario on Dundas Street. I had known Jack for many years, from the time when he opened his gallery to the Ontario Society of Artists for their fall exhibition of small pictures. I approached him diffidently about giving me a show. Jack came to the house, saw what I was doing, and agreed, with the suggestion that he was tired of paintings that were geared for the space above a Rosedale mantel. "I'll paint large if you will sell them," I assured him. This was for me an exciting challenge. I had produced my president's picture for the OSA show and a few other large panels during my hard-edge period. They had been stored in the garage for more than ten years, too good to burn or throw out, but in no demand. Now I was proposing to work on the same scale using my new material from the Arctic. And Jack sounded confident of being able to sell them, so that they would not be compounding my storage problem.

Two of the five-by-seven-foot canvases I developed were iceberg fantasies, abstractions and interwoven forms that were intended to capture the experience of an iceberg without being a literal statement. I was using not masonite panels as before in my large work, but good heavy pine stretchers, custom-made (and expensive) with the best grade of heavy canvas. Other large paintings were of villages and mountains and ice floes. This would be a show with new impact, and I was excited by the prospect. But by the time my studio ceiling hangers were full, I had heard the first rumours that all was not well with Jack and his gallery. Before he had given me a firm date for the show, the rumours proved all too true, and the gallery closed.

Here I was again, without a Toronto gallery. This is the artist's nightmare. We are not salesmen, being both too committed to our work to be objective and too vulnerable to criticism or even indifference to be able to sustain it without great pain. But if you want to be an artist you have to grit your teeth and tackle the ordeal, however you may feel inside. I packed a box of slides and called in at the Merton Gallery because D. Mackay Houstoun, who had preceded me as president of the OSA, had some connection with that gallery, and at least my name would be known there. Jean Johnson, the manager, was pleasant, if non-committal, and promised to "let me know." After a day had passed, I decided that I couldn't wait in suspense any longer. I can still feel the relief I knew when I telephoned for a verdict and heard Jean say, "We are very excited about them." It was a heart-warming response.

The Merton Gallery proved to be an excellent location, thoroughly professional in appearance, and spacious enough for my new large canvases. During my first show there the CBC filmed an interview with me that they aired on television off and on for several years. From Newfoundland to the Yukon I met people afterwards who recognized me from seeing me on *Take Thirty*.

That spring saw my elevation to full member of the Royal Canadian Academy, with one of my iceberg fantasies accepted as my diploma piece.

8

Heart of a Painter

JOHN SCULLION WAS once more promoted and moved, this time to Inuvik up in the Western Arctic. Once again he invited Barbara Greene and me to come and paint. Both of us were always ready for a new experience, and we both said yes. In June of 1977 we flew out to Edmonton on the first leg of our trip. That flight saw a chance meeting that appreciably changed the rest of my life.

Bar had been down the aisle to the back of the aircraft, where she recognized one of our old students from the art department at Central Tech. She came back to me to report. Did I remember Wendy Laughlin? I did remember Wendy, a good student but one who had dropped out sometime in her second year. What was she doing now? And where was she going?

Wendy herself appeared before Bar had had a chance to enlarge, a tall good-looking girl with large grey eyes and a mop of curls around a wide smile. She was on her

way back to Jasper, where she lived, after her wedding
to Dwain Wacko (*Wacko*?), whom she had met while
working as a ski instructor in Jasper. Dwain was a skier,
a mountain climber, and manager of the movie house in
Jasper, which was owned by his mother. Where were we
going and why?

As soon as we told her, Wendy urged us to come to
Jasper to paint. She glowed with enthusiasm for its
beauties. She was still paying rent on the little apartment
that she had lived in before her marriage, and we could
have it free until the end of the month. We could use her
van. She would come and paint with us. She would show
us all the best places. Bar and I were a bit wary about
Inuvik as a sketching ground, so we warned her not to
press her invitation too warmly unless she meant it.
Wendy sparkled at the very possibility that we might
come, wrote down her address and telephone number,
and left us infected by her excitement and charmed by
her.

Being with the Scullions was happiness enough, and
reconciled us to the dusty roads, the brashness of a new
town, the flatness of the delta of the Mackenzie River. We
were still within tree-line, but the trees were the shabbi-
est, raggedest, scrawniest spruce we had ever seen. John
managed to put us on medical or administrative flights to
such Inuit settlements as Holman Island, Pawlutuk, and
Sacks Harbour. Those were high days. We went on a
funeral flight to Aklavik, the old village that Inuvik had
been designed to replace. We always managed at least one
sketch at each place we visited, but after two weeks we
felt that we had exhausted our interest in the flat Western
Arctic, and we phoned Wendy.

Two nights later she met us with open arms as we stepped off the bus in Jasper. Dwain, quiet and detached, hefted our gear into the van and saw us off with Wendy to the apartment that she had vacated when she married. It was pretty well stripped of furniture. There was a thin pad, wide enough for two, on the floor of one bedroom, which Wendy had made attractive (she hoped) with pillows and sheets and a blanket. In the kitchen she had set up a card table and two straight chairs, and brought a kettle, some dishes, and cutlery for two. There were bits and pieces in the refrigerator. Was there anything else we would need? We thanked her, assured her that it was all just fine, and saw her off home. It was then past midnight. Bar and I looked at each other and as one voice said emphatically, "I'm not sleeping with *you*."

This was the summer I was having all the so-called arthritis trouble, feeling my age. Without apology I accepted the thin pad, and doubled it. Bar settled into the other bedroom on the floor. The moans and groans as we struggled up in the morning were comic but sincere. We ate well enough, trust Bar for that, but there was no place to be comfortable. When I wanted to relax for a few minutes, I sat on the floor, leaning against my bedroll, and sipped neat rye.

Wendy entertained us in the small flat where she and Dwain were beginning married life, and was a delightful painting companion when she managed to come with us.

The next time I saw Wendy was in February, when I flew west to have a week in the Gallie ski chalet at Lake Louise with Fran Bennett and her mother and younger sister, Susan. More than ten years had passed since

Frannie had lived with me. Those years had brought her a failed marriage and more than one unsatisfactory "relationship." Her family had come east again and were living in Meaford, a hundred miles north of Toronto. Fran was estranged from them, and Madeline grieved. A painting trip with me was the carrot that we dangled in front of Fran to bring her from San Francisco to be with us. Madeline and I hoped that it would break a spell and coax Fran out of her alienation from her family.

There was magic in that week. Fran discovered a talent she had never suspected, and went back to San Francisco to enrol in an art school. Young Susan was a cheerful lubricant who defused the tensions that occasionally built. Wendy came down from Jasper for a few days, and she and Fran and I had wonderful sessions out in the sunny snow trying to capture the mountains in deep winter. It accomplished more than Madeline and I had dared to hope.

Then came my last Merton show. After it closed, Jean Johnson left and went to new responsibilities at Harbourfront. The reorganization of the gallery eliminated a manager, and I was once more on the search. This time I approached the Aggregation Gallery down on Front Street. It was considered to be progressive, honest, and discriminating, and I remembered working with David Tuck of that gallery when I was chairing the art committee at the Ontario Institute for Studies in Education. David served as one of the acquisition advisers, and I had found him perceptive and dependable. My experience with the Merton had given me a little more confidence to help me approach him. David introduced his partner,

Lynne Wynick, and together they chose a few paintings to "try out on their clientele." Then all was silence for several months.

It was about then that Wendy and Dwain were in Toronto on a visit and came to Fool's Paradise for dinner. It was night, the fire was glowing, the lamps making pools of light about the room, and Dwain and Wendy were talking about Jasper Park and its tourists, how much they wished they had a film to show them on rainy afternoons that would give them the park as the climbers and skiers know it. They wanted to make a picture themselves since there was none to buy or rent. Why not? It sounded like a terrific idea. We tossed it about some more that night.

A few months later, while Dwain was off on an all-male canoe trip into some northern wilderness, Wendy got busy and rounded up half a dozen businessmen who were willing to put up some money for such a venture. Wendy was young and ingenuous-looking, with a little-girl voice that was deceptively gentle. I suspect that she roused the protective male in her investors. Besides, she knew the park, she knew the boredom of the tourists in bad weather and that the theatre was there idling away every afternoon. How could she fail? By the time Dwain returned, she had so many commitments that Dwain panicked and pulled out so that his little theatre would not be at risk.

Wendy was in reality as gentle as a bulldozer. She drove on. The saga of that pioneer film deserves its own book. She was exploited and robbed by her first director and crew, given the facts of life in the film industry by a stranger with whom she chanced to share a taxi in New York, met a world-champion white-water kayak team who provided the climax of her story on a mountain stream never before navigated by kayak or anything else, and ended up in debt (what else) but with an award-winning hour-long documentary.

I flew out for the opening in Jasper, a glamorous affair that parodied Hollywood, with line-ups around the block for both showings, a standing ovation in the theatre as the credits rolled, many of us in tears, and a super-party at the high school afterwards, with all the speeches and bouquets one could wish. It is proof of Wendy's inexperience that it was only after the film was finished that she went off to Cannes and other film festivals to try to sell it and earn back the money that had gone into it.

Wendy had tasted blood. She had learned so much. It could never be so hard again. Would I let her make a film of my life and work? By this time she was convinced that I was a great artist, under-recognized. I couldn't help but agree to the under-recognized, and it was pleasant to hear that I was a great artist, and besides, I love to act. So yes, of course. I would be delighted if she made such a film. This was as far as we had come when the city of Scarborough presented me with its civic Award of Merit at a very pleasant ceremony, at which I made a short speech of acceptance. In faith that there would be a film in which to use the footage, Wendy sent a cameraman and soundman to record the moment.

The next filming was at the opening of my first solo show at the Aggregation Gallery. Lynne and David had observed the feedback after some of my work had been shown for several months, and I was in. We have never looked back. They took me into the select company of their artists because they judged me to be the best in my field, their criterion for choosing any artist. They consider me to have expanded the tradition of Canadian landscape painting by virtue of what they call my strong individual statement and by my use of abstraction to interpret my personal response to nature. That first exhibition with them was pure pleasure for me. It was the first time a gallery had taken the responsibility of framing and pricing off my hands and had looked after all the details of designing the invitation and hanging the show. I was consulted, but also advised, and recognized how good the advice was.

The morning of the opening Richard Leiterman, whom Wendy by great good fortune had secured as director of the McCarthy film, was at the gallery, making careful records of the canvases on the wall and then mingling with the crowds that came, picking up bits of conversation with former students, friends, and collectors. The shots of me that were kept in by the editor are a comfort to me. I look relaxed and comparatively young. A year later, when the film was being completed, I had aged twenty-five years.

A month after that opening I was on my way west with Nan and Barbara Greene in a huge RV – short for recreational vehicle, a misnomer in this case. There was very little recreational about that trip. It began to snow before we were fifty miles up the Trans-Canada, and after the second night our water pipes and sewage system were frozen solid, the supplementary battery run down, and the van was slipping and skidding over iced and snowy roads towards Thunder Bay and sanctuary at Susan Ross's house. The hill down to her place was a gentle slide,

but we managed to stop at the door. We abandoned the
RV to the snow that was blotting out the sky, and bolted
inside. I had chosen April for our trip because it would
be spring, but the joke was not just on me.

Susan, as usual, was all warm hospitality, and kept us
until the storm had blown itself out and the roads were
ploughed again – and until I had slipped while shovelling
out the back of the van, sprained my knee, been taken
down to emergency at the local hospital, and been
equipped with crutches so that I could move about.
Fortunately, it was the left knee, and the van was an
automatic.

The next complication was twenty-four-hour stomach
flu, which hit us one after another, mercifully a day apart.
Nan's bed at the back made an excellent hospital for
whoever was sunk in misery that day.

The farther west we went, the more the weather improved, but not enough to thaw us out. I have a vivid
memory of lying on my side on a snowy road in Saskatchewan, head under the back of the van, using a screw-
driver as a chisel and hammering it into the ice at the end
of the dump pipe, hoping in vain to start it flowing and
empty the van's meagre holding tank, all of us laughing
at the absurdity of our dilemma. The next day we reached
the badlands of southern Saskatchewan and reported to
the Dawson Ranch, which Dalton Muir had told us was
the only means of access to the best area for painting.

On the Dawson Ranch we were given western hospitality, but no access. Too much snow had made the roads
impassable. Mr. Dawson hitched a team of big brown
work-horses to a long sleigh, piled on it square bales of
hay for us to sit against, and drove us half a mile across

snowy fields to the lip of the canyon, where we could look down on the drama of the rough eroded forms. The farm collie leapt and gambolled beside us as we jerked and jingled along behind the horses. By the time we were back at the Dawson house, the van, sitting over an oil heater in the big farm machinery shed, was thawed, and we still hope that our sewage was an acceptable contribution to the fertility of the field outside.

We were due to meet Wendy and her film crew at Brooks, Alberta, twenty or so miles short of Dinosaur Provincial Park, so that our actual arrival at the park, and our first reaction to its challenge, could be caught on camera. Being unable to paint in the Saskatchewan badlands as planned gave us four days to use, enough for a taste of prairie painting that turned out to be a real plus. It also gave us our first incidents of engine failure.

Apparently the make of engine in our RV was notorious for the bad habits of its automatic choke, as one of our several generous amateur or professional Samaritans explained to us. Bar is mechanical, the one who just naturally takes over coping with a temperamental refrigerator or furnace. She taught me to help her loosen the right screws to remove the engine casing in the cab of the van so that she could operate the choke by hand while I started the engine and kept it going. We became quite good at it.

But we couldn't do it ourselves when a brake disc failed at Brooks. We were in a garage there, immobilized, waiting for a part to come from Calgary, when Wendy and the film crew arrived. This was when I first saw Wendy the producer, the organizer. She was not keeping a film crew idle and on salary while we waited for a

delivery from Calgary! By the time she had telephoned
for a courier in Calgary to bring us the part as fast as a
truck could burn up the road, the local man had located
a salvaged part in Brooks and was busy installing it. By
morning we were back on schedule, with the sound-man
and a cameraman immortalizing us in the van while we
worked at keeping the chit-chat light and plausible as we
rolled along the highway towards Dinosaur Park.

Wendy had another chance to use her skills when we
arrived there. The park superintendent flatly refused to
let the film crew do its work. He had had some bitter
experience not long before with a commercial film outfit
that had driven horses up and down his beautiful fragile
hills and done irreparable damage. No more. He would,
however, let her use his telephone to get in touch with his
boss in Ottawa, and a couple of hours later, after much
persuasion and many personal testimonials from influen-
tial people, Wendy had his permission, which became less
and less grudging as he observed our meticulous respect
for the landscape, the palaeontological finds, and the
exhibits. Wendy's sweetness and genuine concern won
him completely, and after the filming was done and the
crew departed, Bar and Nan and I became practically
honoured guests, with our van plugged in to the staff
house, and permission to go beyond the public areas to
paint.

The next month Wendy and Richard and I flew to
England, courtesy of British Airways. What is more, we
flew first class. I wallow in that memory sometimes,
savouring again the champagne, the roast lamb with the
juices running out, the exquisite attentions. It is pleasant
to have experienced such luxury once.

After we arrived, our working hours were too rigorous for either sleep or meals. We were usually due on location by five or six in the morning. Before traffic builds up is the best time in London. By mid-morning we had been at work for hours. But I was very happy. To be in my beloved London, with no responsibility except to do as I was told, stand here, walk there, sit in this park or in that pub and answer the questions I was asked, was bliss.

Wendy and I each had a very personal thrill. For me it was to be back in the Central School of Arts and Crafts, where Nory and George and I had studied over forty-five years earlier, actually in the very painting studio where I had drawn from the nude model and agonized over the criticisms of the teachers. For Wendy the high spot was our filming morning at Stonehenge. She had been excited by what she had learned about it in my history of art class when she had been a student at CTS, and had made up her mind to see it for herself. But since those days Stonehenge had become an endangered species, and she was assured that it would take at least six months to get through the red tape that protected it. Wendy just smiled gently, and in a day had managed to secure written permission.

Since we were to film the sunrise, we stayed at Salisbury the night before, in one of the lovely ancient inns near the cathedral. But lovely or not, Richard's wake-up call at 3:45 A.M. went to the wrong room, where it was very ill received. Richard therefore overslept, made a late start, drove like a fiend (although he managed to miss the rabbit that leapt out at us), and ran out of gas as the car neared the Stonehenge parking lot. We pushed it the rest of the way. The night watchman refused to believe that Wendy's letter meant what it said, and tried to keep us outside the fence that surrounds the stone circle. It took all Wendy's feminine charm and Alberta stubbornness to lick that one, but she was not turning back then. And there we were, inside the sacred ruins, ready with the camera as the sun opened a red eye above the far slope, and able to get such a leisurely sequence of me strolling among the megaliths that no one could guess I was chilled to the marrow and would need twenty minutes in a hot bath up to my neck before I stopped shaking.

Before June, when we were due for filming in the Arctic, Wendy's plans were overtaken by a recession, and one of her major investors backed out. It was a great disappointment to all of us, including Dwain, who had been booked as cameraman for that adventure. We settled instead for a few days in the studio at the Knothole on Georgian Bay, with Dwain and Wendy living in her father's motor home close to the cottage, and Richard and Margaret, his wife, staying at a motel in nearby Nobel. Ginny faded tactfully out of the studio where I was to be filmed at work, helped Wendy and Margaret organize food for all of us, and shared the cookouts at the fireplace on the rocks when the day's work was done.

The real meat of the finished film, to my mind, is the record of the hour-by-hour work of painting a badlands canvas, which I did that week, thinking out loud as I worked, with the camera observing the steps and the sound equipment recording my thoughts. It was one of the most gruelling experiences of my life, but I believed that it would be worthwhile, so I was willing. I was amazed at my own vulnerability. In retrospect, the silence of the film crew, who were all friends by this time, was respectful. But nobody said that the painting was coming along well, or that he liked it. Even Ginny didn't comment. I became more and more insecure, convinced that it was a disaster but committed to slugging away at it. The haggard lines in my face in the studio sequences reveal my tension. The afternoon that I finished the painting I knew that I was not satisfied with the form in the lower right-hand corner, but I had covered the canvas, and I was utterly exhausted. The painting and I were both done.

Richard had some details to tidy up the next morning, after which he and Margaret stretched a blanket out in the sunshine on the rocks and had a few hours' relaxation. Wendy and Dwain had driven off in their van. Ginny began a fundamental reorganization of the kitchen to recover control of the refrigerator that she had been sharing with two other women, and I picked things up and put them down again. When, finally, the Leiterman car had disappeared over the rocks, I had myself a quiet nervous breakdown. I think I lay down and read a whodunnit. We played Scrabble in the afternoon, sinful dissipation. It was a full week before I could bear to look at my badlands canvas again to revise the passage that I had known was wrong.

Wendy was still in financial difficulties, and while she was struggling to find the resources to go on, she lost Richard. He had to accept other work, and was off out of the country. This meant a switch in directors half-way through, but I was not inconsolable. I had begun to be very uneasy about the person that I felt was emerging from Richard's film. Was I really a contemplative? Did I drift dreamily along, brooding about the nature of art? Peter Shatalow, the new, younger, and less experienced director, was willing to listen to my misgivings, and I thank him for his skilful editing that used Richard's rushes to build a much more plausible me than I had feared.

There was one large segment of the photography still to come. It was decided to create a dinner-party at Fool's Paradise to be the umbrella under which everything else sheltered. Wendy and Peter agreed that the conversation that occurred spontaneously would be used to tie the sequences together. Nan was to be a guest. The others, although acquaintances, had never before been entertained in my home. Wendy also agreed that I should be relieved of worries about food, and Marjorie Dickinson, my friend of Sunday-morning breakfasts at Nan's, was taken on staff as caterer. Peter wanted to use the daytime for photographing the paintings and archival snapshots that were in the attic and storage cupboards at Fool's Paradise, but I balked. There was no way I could have a dinner-party at night if the house was crawling with cameramen and other technicians, lights, cables, and confusion during the day. When I have a party, I do everything possible ahead of time, so that I can greet my guests in serenity, with the food under control, the living-room polished, the fire laid, the table set, the cats fed.

I still laugh at the memory of the day of that dinner-party. Wendy and Peter had agreed to stay out of the house and to film the camping-in-the-woods sequence, the arrival of the truck with the lumber for the house, and the beginning of the building of Fool's Paradise. Instead of the film crew and my paintings in confusion in the house, I had the actress who was playing me as a young woman, the truck driver, and the film crew too, whenever they needed to warm up out of the raw December wind outside. My one bathroom was in constant use. I spent much of the day fitting the actress with the clothes I had actually worn or might have worn, hauling up from the cellar or down from the attic the camping gear for the outdoor fire and for putting up the tent. The studio and the hallways were knee-deep in cables and all the equipment needed for the filming outside and in the living-room, where the dinner table was set. My kitchen was the film crew's canteen. The miracle was that in spite of the confusion, by the time the actors had gone and I had wriggled into evening dress, after the guests had arrived and we had all chatted around the fire and warmed up physically and socially, the good food and wine stimulated some real talk at the dinner table. I could even forget the cameraman beside me and ignore the floodlights.

The little fragment of film that Wendy and Peter chose to use at the end, and to freeze behind the credits, was a minute or so of me skating on the pond. We had planned to go to the indoor rink, not far away, but December had turned so cold that the pond froze. It was a far more attractive background. The crew was here: why not use the pond? We found out why after everything was set up. The cameraman went right through the ice. Time out while he pulls off his wet boots and is fitted with something warm and dry. I am much lighter than he is. Will it take my weight? I try it cautiously, and it seems firm enough. The sequence was filmed on the far side of the pond beyond the hole in the ice, and I was torn between feeling that a shot of me falling in would have added a touch of hilarity, and relief that the ice held.

Wendy and I shared three exciting previews of the film,

which was finally named *Doris McCarthy – Heart of a Painter*. The first, in Toronto at the St. Lawrence Centre to a packed house, was the best of all for me because of the friends and family. Everyone was there, from every corner of my life. Frances Dafoe, an old student and former world-champion figure skater, laughed so hard at the McCarthy spiral that she wept.

A few weeks later the Alberta Department of Culture sponsored a showing in New York at the Institute of the Americas and mounted a solo show of my paintings at the same time, with a reception that did us proud. And finally it was screened at Canada House in London, and again was very well received. (We had tried to arrange an exhibition to accompany it there but had been turned down, which made it doubly ironic to have everyone asking us why there were none of my paintings in the gallery or even on the walls of the reception rooms.) Both the CBC and TV Ontario have used the film in prime time more than once.

To me it has been a marvellous support. These days I am often asked to speak to art groups or cultural organizations, and when I am, I say, "Yes, if you will show the film and let me answer questions." It is a good film that stands up even after repeated viewings, and I can still enjoy it. Like most works of art, it is not perfect. I see a few flaws that I would love to correct, but it has good pace, never loses its audience, says most of the things I would like to tell a group, and says them well. Bless Wendy for it. Bless her anyhow.

9

A Life of Holiness

AFTER MY RETIREMENT from teaching I scheduled my major painting trips for early spring or fall; the summer months were sacred to the cottage at Georgian Bay with Ginny. We had found our life there offered the best period of uninterrupted work in the whole year. No two years were ever identical, perhaps no two weeks, but life there had a consistency that was very precious.

The deep bay that isolates our peninsula from the adjoining mainland is known as the Keyhole from its shape, and the largest of the cottages, which is closest to it, we call the Keyhole. Ginny's and mine is known as the Knothole because it is *not* the Keyhole, and it is more rustic. The third cottage, out of sight beyond the big point, is the smallest of the three, and seems well described as the Cubby Hole. Ginny's brother named the high place that overlooks us Ben Hole, and the arm of rock that stretches out into the bay is Holy Point. As soon

as Christmas is over, the thought of the cottage is a secret
warmth inside, and settling in to our weeks there is a
sharp joy.

One of the constant pleasures of life at the cottage is
the pine-carpeted path to the privy. Overnight the spiders
will have stretched webs from side to side, and the sun
catches them just before they catch me in the face. No
matter how thorough my sweep-out of the privy yesterday, I never get rid of the spiders, but last year I did
regretfully take down the heap of dried leaves and grasses
that was always on the shelf inside the door. For two years
a red squirrel lived in that nest, and when surprised at
night would lean out with his black button eyes and then
scurry along the top of the door and up over the roof.
Through the screen of pines and cedar undergrowth I can
see the colour of the dawn sky and know if it will be a fair
day.

It is a good morning when I have wakened before the
sun comes up over the trees on the eastern shore of the
bay. At this hour I can be leisurely about the coffee that
I take back to bed, sipping it slowly and staring between
sips. The sky is gradually gaining colour above the heat
haze that dims the far shore and the distant islands. A
song sparrow flits on to the brush pile beside the stone
fireplace on the rocks and opens beak and throat in a
burst of "Dee-dee-dee – tra-lip tra-pitee tra-la-la." I
watch a tubular brown mole scud from under the brush
across the open rock into the sanctuary of the mossy
hollow where the iris and the St. John's wort grow and
bloom. The gulls that were laughing and screaming at
dawn have gone fishing, but a sandpiper lands on their
favourite rock island, the half-submerged giant lying just

off the shore. I watch him bob his way along the water's
edge up to the giant's head. Is it shad flies he's finding?
There goes our resident beaver, a brown head leaving a
silver wake as he glides smoothly past, off to work in the
beaver meadow beyond the blasted channel, no doubt.
He comes back to his home in the Keyhole bay at dusk
every evening like a city commuter. Thinking about his
work day reminds me of mine, and I take the hint and
drop my feet out of bed.

I hang up my nightgown, wrap the big towel around
me, slide into my sandals, and pick up facecloth and soap
on my way to the place where the rock goes smoothly off
into deep water. Holding soap and facecloth high, I venture one step into the wet – and slide the rest of the way.
It's always comic when I find myself helpless to stop until
I have reached deep water or fallen with a great splash
on the slippery ledge beside the rock that I use to pull
myself out with. I soap, rinse, and wallow, luxuriating in
the sweet cold water. At this hour I have the bay to myself.
Virginia is probably awake but never admits it until I am
dressed, with my bed made. She moves only when she
hears the wind-chimes on the clothesline ring out as I jerk
them in hanging up my towel.

The cabin is tidied for the day, both beds orderly in
their day covers, and the breakfast table inviting when
we sit down together. I wait for Virginia's daily "I'm not
awake yet," a ritual opening. After that I talk for both of
us, reviewing the night, reporting the heron or other
incidents of my coffee hour, commenting on the weather
prospects of the day, no answer demanded. I clear the
table and leave her sitting over her second cup of tea. It

is still just after eight o'clock, and my morning is off to a good start.

The studio greets me with its familiar smell of sun-baked cedar and turpentine. The big canvas of Glacier Bay that I was working on yesterday confronts me from the easel. I open up my aluminum armchair, make myself comfortable in front of it, and look about me.

Any duck families on the bay this morning? The islands and the far shore are clearing. But I am here to get to work. So how does the glacier look twelve hours later?

In June of 1987 Bobs Haworth and I had gone west by train and up the inland passage to Alaska and the Yukon. It was a proper cruise, very luxurious and very expensive, but Peter had died the year before and Bobs badly needed something to look forward to. After Peter's death she had had major surgery and was far too frail for my usual standard of travel. Most of her friends considered her "difficult," and Bobs herself was in some doubt how she could adapt to sharing a room with another woman. But she was determined that I should not regret taking her, and I was determined that she should have a wonderful experience. It was a good basis for success. The high spot for me had been our day-long cruise in Glacier Bay, where I had taken slides and made many quick sketches but had had no opportunity to do any real painting. To capture that rare day on canvas was a terrific challenge.

The composition is still all right. I like the way it pulls your eye from the cloud-hung mountain down at an angle, and twists you again into the foreground. The movement of the river of ice pouring down towards you is interest-ing, and the quicker rhythm of the jagged little ice floes in the foreground is fun. But the near hill on the right seems a bit aggressive. Does that mean that the tone contrast is too strong? Let me lighten it.

My palette is laid out from yesterday, but I check to be sure that all the colours are in good supply and reach for a tube of white and start to unscrew the top before I remember gloves. Damn! I can't get used to having to wear them. Allergies are a curse. Oh well. Special hand cream first, hands waved in the air to speed drying, rubber gloves that I peeled off last night blown right side out and pulled on, painting apron tied around, and now, at last, the tube of white again.

The next time I leave the glacier is when the wheeze of the hand-pump at the back door and the ring of the pot lid tell me that Ginny has finished in the kitchen and is putting washing to soak in the big pot on the washstand outside. Half an hour later she is at her own easel beside her own stretch of windows facing the bay. If she comments on my work, it is a good sign, and I go on with renewed confidence. We are supportive of each other. But if there is silence, I look more critically at what I am doing. Sometimes I will ask for an opinion, sometimes set my teeth and press doggedly on. After a bit I realize that I have been whistling the same fragment of something or other all morning. "Sorry," I mutter. "Just change it," she suggests gently, and I do, at least temporarily.

We break to split a beer sometime during the morning. Today it is cool enough to enjoy the sun, so we sit up on the rocks in front of the cottage. The cedar chairs stay out all summer, and I observe that last year's stain is holding up well. As outside maintenance man it is my job to keep an eye on such things. Chippie runs out from between

two of the fireplace rocks and sits, hand on heart, observing us. I go in to get some peanuts for him, but he is off
before I return. We put a few on the coffee table to tempt
him back, and settle in to enjoy the gulls, the movement
of the water against the shore, the launches coming down
the channel from Parry Sound, the wind surfers, and any
signs of life we can observe around the cottages on the
far shore or on the islands. Ginny, who is using water-colour, decides that her work will be dry enough to go on
with by now, and I return eagerly to the glacier.

By lunch-time it is too hot on the rocks. I move the
table and we carry the tray and our chairs to the shade of
the grove of pin-cherry trees in front of the studio, and
watch the barn swallows feeding their young in the nest
under the eaves. Those big red mouths! How do the
parents keep track of which ones get fed each time?

Then back into the gloves and the apron for another
couple of hours in Alaska. At least twice during the
afternoon we have to carry out a bee-rescue operation.
The silly things will zoom in the big barn door at the back
that we throw open when the studio heats up in the
afternoon. They buzz frantically against the window, and
one of us has to use the glass jar and the piece of cardboard to trap each one and let it loose at the other door,
to watch it disappear in an arc over the roof of the cottage.
When the sun has moved so far around that it is starting
to come in the big back door, I remember to look at my
watch. Almost four o'clock and time to stop.

The clean-up is good for another half-hour. Brushes
are so precious that to keep them soft and responsive I
am willing to go through the whole process every day,
turps to get the paint out, more fresh turps, still more fresh

turps, with the hairs pulled gently away from their ends across clean rag or paper towel, warm water and soap next to get every trace of turps out of the brush, washing and rewashing, separating the hairs with gentle fingers to be sure that no paint is lurking at the top. When the brush at last smells of soap and not of turps, I can give it a couple of final rinses and know that tomorrow it will be like a new brush. And so off with the gloves for another day.

Our official working day ends at four o'clock, when our friends from the other two "holes" join us for tea. The way everything is held in partnership gives us a sense of being a family, and we cherish the social times. I carry enough chairs and the tea table to the sheltered side of the house. Ginny has the big tray set with everything needed and the kettle almost at the boil as our friends drift in. Tea is welcome and the home-made cookies appreciated, but the real attraction is the hour of reading together afterwards. When the day's chit-chat is slowing and the blue china mugs have been refilled all around, the first reader starts.

We have tried quite a variety of books in the last few years, from Frye's *The Great Code* to a P.D. James mystery. Recently we had a go at Dorothy L. Sayers's *The Mind of the Maker*. There are good critical capacities in the group, and some experience in thinking theologically and philosophically. When we are discussing something like Sayers's chapter about free-will and miracle, it is far too soon that someone remembers the time and we break for the day, still arguing.

Ginny is chief chef. While I wash up the tea mugs, her head is in the refrigerator, setting in motion her well-organized plans for a good dinner. This is my hour for what

I call road-work, cutting dead limbs from trees, pruning
lower branches to coax a tree to grow higher, shaping and
changing. Today I am going to look for a big flat rock to
widen the front step at the Keyhole. I take the precaution
of changing from sandals to rubber boots. The rock I find
is a segment cracked loose when the Hydro workers
blasted to instal our pole. The back of it is buried in moss
and earth that I must scrape away to see just how big it
is. There is an overhang on one edge that will give me a
chance to get a lever under it. The wrecking bar won't do,
too small, rock too heavy. But this six-foot length of
two-by-four, with a rock as a fulcrum, lets me lift it an
inch or so. If I sit on the end of the two-by-four to hold it
down and the rock up, I can use the rake to push a small
stone under the edge. That will hold it up while I reposi-
tion the lever and pry the big rock up high enough to get
the end of one of the rollers under it. My rollers are
lengths of firewood and not as smooth as I wish. I repeat
the process, shoving, putting all my weight on the end of
my two-by-four, getting the rollers under, inch by inch,
until I can begin to think of coaxing the big rock to move
forward. That is enough for one day. I am steaming hot.
I drop tools where they are, ready for tomorrow, and back
at the cottage peel my sticky clothes off my wet back,
wrap the big towel about me, and make for the bay.

The clean cool water! But it takes several duckings and
sloshings before I stop tasting the salt. Today I soap my
hair too, and lie back feeling the little waves rinsing it for
me. Ginny has the pots bubbling and a drink in her hand
by the time I am dressed, but there's still time for a quick
one for me.

We take dinner seriously, with the table formally set,

with slender pine trees beyond the window instead of candles and ripening grasses and mulleins outside as our floral decoration. On the table itself we use the lovely old blue-flowered china that came with the cottage, and our own sparkling glasses. The vegetable garden is producing well this year, beet greens and snow peas already, and the first of the tomatoes, red as a Fort McMurray hard hat. My elderberry wine is a contralto note in the symphony of colour. After dinner Ginny pours herself another glass of it while I look after the washing up and carry the bowl of kitchen scraps over to the compost pile beside the garden.

The sun is low by now, sending long shadows across the rocks, catching the brilliant white of the gulls riding in the bay, reflecting back from windows on the far islands. We set out on our evening walk, choosing the shore route rather than the road to the post-box this time. The water level has dropped, uncovering broad ledges of rock, leaving puddles that we can explore. Tonight, for the first time this season, we can get dry-shod to the end of Holy Point. The gulls fly off screaming as we approach. Purple splotches on the rocks tell us that they have been raiding the blueberry bushes. Having explored the point in detail, we turn inland, up through the juniper bushes, past the grove of big pines, where Flo's niece pitched her tent last year, up the long spine of glacier-scraped granite that leads to the high place where the three pines guard Marjorie's ashes. On the way up the slope, in the little hollows where dust has gathered and made soil, tall grasses are turning gold, moving in the breeze like the flaxen hair of the goosegirl in the fairy-tale.

At the top of the hill we settle. I lie on the sun-warmed

rock with my head propped on the driftwood log that we
rolled into position up there years ago. Ginny sits beside
me on the thickest part of the log, from which arthritic
knees have less difficulty getting up. We are monarchs
surveying our kingdom. Rock by rock, tree by tree, we
approve it. Each of the three hydro poles has its own
herring gull on top. Good. Joe, our permanent resident
ringbill, is patrolling in front of the cottage, screaming
protest at any other gull who drifts in and driving him off.
Good. We watch a family of mergansers scramble up on
to the giant and settle into a tight cluster around mother,
whose head flicks back and forwards in vigilance before
she too settles for the night. Good.

When the sun drops out of sight below the woods
behind us and Ginny slaps the first mosquito, I take it as
a cue. Our return to the cottage is direct. This is the
moment we have been waiting for, and we waste no time.
I carry the lamp to the table while Ginny brings the
Scrabble box. She lays things out deftly. The poor board
is shabby, stained with blood from many mosquitoes,
worn with years of use. The box is falling apart, but it is
precious because in the lid we have kept a record of the
biggest scores and unusual plays. We fish out last night's
score-paper, on which there is still space.

"Let's hope I don't have another run of vowels," says
Ginny. "None at all is just as bad," I reply.

We play sociable Scrabble, each of us more interested
in high scores than in competition. If the board becomes
too strangled, or one of us is stuck, she spreads out the
letters and we both study them to find a play. Our
satisfaction with a full seven-letter word is mutual.
Tonight is notable because I manage to get the word

"eczema" on a triple for the very good score of sixty, and Ginny, who has been holding her breath while I decide where to play, lets out a cry of triumph because "warding," the seven-letter word she was hoping to be able to play, can join with my *a* to become "awarding," an eight-letter word that adds up to a score of eighty.

Once in bed Ginny is apt to read longer than I. When the words begin to run together or I find my eyes closing over my book, I know I am done. "Goodnight, dear. Sleep well," I manage, as I turn out my light. Sometimes I know when hers goes off, sometimes not. For all such days, and all the gifts that they have held, thank God, Amen.

Of course there was the year that Ginny broke her ankle and lay helpless on the path behind the Knothole until she could be helped to crawl to the car on hands and one knee. The Parry Sound Hospital, on that one occasion, did a poor job of setting the break, and three days later I drove her down to Toronto, in great pain, to have it taken out of the cast and redone completely. The surgeon said that putting the fragments of bone together was like sorting cornflakes. But her brother Ed drove her back ten days later, and she enjoyed the rest of the summer on crutches. And then there were two summers when dear Ed was with us in a wheelchair after the stroke that had left him paralysed on one side. Those were good days, but we would not want them back. And for the last few years Flo has been with Mary in the Cubby Hole, so nearly blind that she can no longer walk across the rocks to the Knothole without guidance, and has had to put away her paints. Worse than that, she can no longer play Scrabble.

Yvonne and Ginny and I, in recognition of the realities of our ages, have invited one of Flo's nieces and her husband to come in with us as partners. They already know and love the place. This year Joe, the banded gull, was missing from the rocks and his patrol taken over by a strange ringbill, who we must admit is somewhat more amiable a bird than Joe. Only the rocks do not change, or so slowly that the lichen seems always to have been there and the waves that wash the shore eternal.

10

Developments

IF THE SUMMERS AT the Keyhole seem to exist in a world of unchanging rock blessed by sun and rain and winds, where growth is slow and change is gradual, it is not so of life in the rest of my world.

Art galleries live in a state of flux. After my two exhibitions with John Robertson in Ottawa, he sold his establishment and I moved to the Wells Gallery. Barbara Wells had been a student at one time in the art department at Central Tech, and operated a fine small business near the Chateau Laurier on Sussex Street. A few years later soaring rents forced her to close, and I took my work out of the city to the Welch Gallery. Malcolm Welch had been John Robertson's accountant, exposed to so much art while working with John that he had become addicted. He built himself a retirement home on the Ottawa River some forty miles north of Ottawa and attached a small gallery to it. This was the beginning of a very happy association and a pattern of annual solo exhibitions. After the Robertsons moved nearby, my weekends with Donna and Malcolm included a reunion with them over dinner at one home or the other.

Malcolm had adventurous, eclectic tastes and was particularly interested in giving young artists their first chance. Fortunately, he forgave me for not being young or avant-garde, and built for me a good following in the district. I would save for him my small water-colours, the quickies and fun sketches. The gallery openings brought out Dalton and Marianne Muir, the Schatskys and many old students and other friends from Ottawa, and the Scullions, Bar Greene, and Madeleine Moir from farther afield.

There was an ache that Peggy and Bora were no longer there. It is the hardest part of growing old that every year some of the people you have loved most and longest are gone forever. Peggy and Bora adopted me when I first moved away from home, encouraged me as a young artist, bought paintings when they were poor and struggling themselves, loved me through their bad times and mine, kept the door open to me when they moved to Ottawa, and were completely unchanged by the dizzy heights to which Bora rose.

The Aggregation Gallery in Toronto was another casualty of rising rent. Twice Lynne Wynick and David Tuck had found inexpensive space in an unfashionable district, opened a gallery, created an ambiance that attracted others to the district, and had the rent jacked up past the point where the gallery could support it. In 1982 they found a much larger place than the old one down on Front Street and changed the gallery name to Wynick/Tuck. The new accommodation on Spadina Avenue had been a

garment factory, spacious but shabby. Not only did
Lynne and David create a beautiful gallery there; they
started a movement that gradually filled the whole ware-
house with art galleries. I think that of all my solo exhibitions, the one that gave me the most personal aesthetic
satisfaction was the first up on the fourth floor of 80
Spadina Avenue. The show was of the Alberta badlands,
almost all oils, with several of the twelve-by-sixteen panels done on the spot and the rest large or very large
canvases painted at the Knothole or in my studio in
Toronto. The paintings were warm in colour, full of
ochres, siennas, and warm whites, and the western sun
streaming in on the freshly sanded floor enhanced the
golden tones of the work. Sales were nothing to boast
about compared to previous shows because Toronto patrons didn't easily relate to the bizarre forms of the
hoodoos and eroded hills of the badlands, but I didn't
care. I knew, and David and Lynne knew that the paintings would sell eventually.

My schedule of exhibitions has been stepped up rather
than diminished recently. But all the pain is gone. The day
I realized that once a painting was put into a frame it could
stay there was a landmark day. No more crawling around
on my knees on the studio floor on Sunday afternoons.
Gallery support has freed me to paint. Lynne and David
take my work, have it framed, choose what to hang, set
the prices, and after consultation with me look after the
invitations. They arrange for shows in galleries in other
cities, pick the works and ship them, and leave it to me
whether or no I will travel to the opening.

My latest luxury is to have Len Deakin, who has been
making my stretchers, also stretch the canvas and apply

the gesso ground. This was a chore that I had done for myself for sixty years, and taught my students to do with pride in the fine taut surface they achieved. Even now it is not to save work that I have resigned the job, but to save time. Days are more precious than ever as the store ahead shrinks.

It was the year of the badlands show that I had a phone call from Fran Bennett in San Francisco with stupendous news. The infant that she had given up for adoption seventeen years before had applied to the Children's Aid to be put in touch with her real mother. Fran had long ago registered with them as willing to be identified. The Children's Aid had notified her, and she was planning to fly to Toronto the next day to meet her daughter at the airport. Could she bring her home to Fool's Paradise for the night? I could hardly believe it, that the ache we had carried in us for seventeen years was to be eased at last.

It was an emotional weekend for everyone. Lorie, as we learned was her name, was in a classic state of teenage rebellion, a school drop-out at grade ten, smoking, drinking, experimenting with drugs and sex, driving her adoptive parents frantic with worry and frustration. Frannie recognized her teenaged self in her daughter, and knew the futility of sermons. She hugged her and let her talk, and I think they went on talking together all night long.

The next day her adopting mother, whose name was also Fran, came for tea, laden with snapshots of Lorie from her exquisite baby days, through the bewitching tot years, and up until you could see the sulks beginning. The two mothers made a valiant effort to like each other and forgive each other – for what? Perhaps for being there. Lorie left us for an hour to go walking with the latest boy-friend, and the talk became freer, with Lorie's mother able to tell Fran some of the heartache she and her husband had been suffering since Lorie had begun to pull away from them in her teens.

The years that followed that strained tea-party were years of growth for everyone. Lorie's adopting father relented on his original "nothing to do with any of them" stance, and the two families recognized that they both cared for Lorie and wanted the best for her. Madeline and Ralph were yearning to know and love this grand-daughter they had never seen. They accepted her whole-heartedly and included her in family gatherings so that she met her whole clan, two uncles and Susan, the aunt who was not far from her in age, and her young cousins. It was two years before her biological father, living out west, was willing to meet her. When that time came, he and his wife, who had known of the illegitimate daughter before they were married, flew east and had a weekend with her. The wife, with extraordinary generosity, left Lorie and her father together, and in a long afternoon of walking beside the lake hand in hand, they fell in love with each other.

Who am I to say what were the strongest factors in the change in Lorie? She went back to school and achieved a senior matriculation in one year, which admitted her to university, although her standing was not high enough for Toronto. By the end of her first year at university she had made the grade that Toronto would accept. She graduated from Toronto with honours. The biggest change that I see is inside her. She has become a warm, outgoing young woman, beautiful not only in her dark hair and her big eyes and her petal skin, but in the person that shines out of the eyes.

I met her real father again and his family at Lorie's wedding not long ago and liked them immensely. I saw the glow of happiness that lit up the adopting parents with pride in the swan that used to be their ugly duckling, and had my own Fran with me at Fool's Paradise, at home, clear-eyed about her daughter, but starry-eyed too, loving her and rejoicing in her happiness.

This October it was Lorie and her young husband who came to Fool's Paradise to make the annual attack on the wild grape that is choking the trees, to cut it off at the root and toss it over the bluffs. It used to be Malcolm Croggon who came every fall for that essential work of maintenance. Seven years after his sudden death I miss him and miss him. But it was great to have these delightful young people this year, to have my brother Douglas join us and share the meal that always celebrates the job accomplished. It adds a special dimension to my pleasure that Lorie's husband is the son of the Tony and Marjorie Darling who often visit Yvonne up at the Keyhole and whom Ginny and I have always liked. Lorie and Tim turn out to be Scrabblers, an additional bond. Tim notes ironically that he is the only person he knows who acquired three mothers-in-law when he married.

These years since I stopped teaching have taken me across Canada fourteen times to paint in Alberta or British Columbia, four times to the Yukon and Alaska or the Western Arctic, five times to Newfoundland or the Maritimes, and seven times to the eastern High Arctic. When I question myself about this wander-pattern, I find that the reasons are complex. The roots of it lie at Haliburton in my earliest days as an artist, when those working holidays with Ethel Curry gave me inspiration, release from the constraints of living with Mother, and the con- genial companionship of a fellow painter. We were fol- lowing the example of Canada's leading artists, and discovering that while travel was good in itself, the best way to experience the places we went to was to paint them. Painting demands a concentration and sensibility that grows into an intimacy with the country, greatly intensifying your awareness of it. You come to know it instead of just seeing it.

After we were earning, we could range farther afield, explore more of Ontario and Quebec, and eventually discover the Gaspé coast. Barachois and its environs became a gathering-place for many of our artist friends and remained for twenty years our favourite summer painting-ground. After retirement and the break-up of the old Gaspé group, I was fortunate to have Nan, Barbara Greene, Audrey Garwood, or some other hard-working congenial artist with me, someone who was still tough enough to survive painting out of doors and enjoy it.

From earliest days I had difficulty in being objective about the models at school, uncomfortable if they looked at my work in case I had made them ugly or failed to capture their personality. This was another attraction of landscape painting; nature didn't talk back. From time to time I painted the men gutting cod at Barachois, roller- skaters in the forties, the games at Arctic Bay, but usually

I used figures as incidents in a landscape, too small to be considered portraits.

Once I had my own home at Fool's Paradise, I had no wish to go anywhere for the sake of getting away, but going away was the price I had to pay for the detachment that would allow me to concentrate on painting. At home I am too busy creating my world. Even the ordinary routine of making my bed and tidying the house every morning is a re-creation of my vision of the serenity and beauty I want for my home. I constantly see something that I can or should do to maintain or enhance that vision. From the melting of the snow until it comes again in December, the garden is eloquent in its plea for attention. I choose to live in a house and I choose to live in Canada and have the drama of the changing seasons, but the cost in terms of shifting furniture, putting summer clothes away and bringing winter woollies down from the attic, cleaning out eavestroughs, and changing from screens to double windows is time. There are some jobs that I can and do delegate. Life has improved since Paula has been coming every third week to clean and polish. It is years now since I have cut my own grass, and every time I drive home I get a sharp pleasure at the seemliness of the neat edges that Greg maintains. Because I want Fool's Paradise to be rural, I won't have the driveway paved, but I see every weed in the gravel that I should pull up to keep it neat. I *see* Fool's Paradise constantly, and with keen pleasure, but it doesn't say "Paint me." It says "Make me more beautiful."

Much as I care about making my home a work of art, I care still more about people, and when someone phones

to ask me to do something, or says, "Will you be at home
if I should come out?" I say "Yes," and I want to be the
kind of person who says yes. The greatest pleasure I have
in Fool's Paradise is the friends who share it, and knowing
that people love to come to it.

A change of scene gives me relief from this pressure
and a great visual stimulus. I am intensely aware of the
world I have moved into and can react to it without
looking at my calendar. Life on location is simple even if
it is not always comfortable. The challenge on a painting
trip is to create the perfection on my panel or canvas. This
demands interpreting, selecting, arranging, ordering, and
changing.

Then how have I managed through the years to get
enough major canvases painted at home? I wait until the
house has been made tight for the winter, and the garden
put to bed. Christmas has been looming on the horizon
like a dark cloud, and I chase that cloud away by getting
the cards designed, printed, addressed, and sent, with
honest-to-goodness notes or even letters. (I have little use
for the kind of card that has only a name.) Gifts are no
longer a nightmare. "Please, nothing that I cannot eat or
drink or burn" is still the rule.

Christmas itself, the festive services, the music and
lights, dinner with all the ceremony and trimmings, is still
a joy, especially when Madeleine Moir or my great-niece
Betsy Jones comes for the holiday. But when it is over
and I have once again restored the living-room to normal,
packed the extra food into the freezer, and Paula has
vacuumed up the pine needles, I move into the studio not
only physically but emotionally, and it becomes for the
next few months the centre of my life.

The technical process of painting a large canvas is not very different from an on-the-spot sketch, except that I usually do my preliminary designing in thin acrylic, using it almost like water-colour. For my first marks on the blank canvas I use a large brush, about an inch wide, flat-ended, with a long handle. After I have made two or three lines to establish essential movement, I walk to the far end of the studio and sit and study it. This is the time to change the proportion of sky to earth, or the placing of a dominant feature. While I am working out the composition, I spend far more time out of reach of the canvas than I do in painting. Sometimes I go into the adjoining kitchen and look through the window into the studio to get even more distance and detachment. When I have made the plan in lines only, and found that it has enough vitality to give me back some excitement, I begin to define dark areas and build up a balance of tone. Soon I am using coloured washes to give local colour and establish the hue of the cast shadows. Local colour is artist's jargon for the colour the object actually is. The colour of the shadows is affected by the colour of the light that hits the object. A warm light will cast a cool shadow, which is why yellow sunlight turns shadows blue, and a cool light will make the shadows appear warm. If an object is lit by a blue light, the shadow side of it and the shadow it casts will both be warm, usually grey with a touch of brown in it.

This is the kind of technical knowledge that is so basic, that I taught to so many generations of students, that I no more think of it while painting than I think about grammar when I am writing. As with perspective, I think of it only when for some reason I decide to defy the rules and create a special tension or element of surprise.

In the studio I use slides freely. The photographs I have taken on location stimulate me the way the original subject did. I use a hand-viewer that is held up to the light. As I look through the viewer with one eye, the other closed, the whole world for me is the slide. I am able to imagine that I am there, seeing that view for the first time. In my mind I react as I would have done on the spot, looking for a feature to be the focus of my attention, observing what can be used as it is and what needs to be moved, or omitted, or changed in size. I may run twenty or thirty slides through the viewer before one gives me the jab in the solar plexus that I recognize as "an idea." Something, a colour, a form, a movement, a pattern, or a mood, will suddenly make me want to paint, and I put that slide to one side. After a bit I go back over the ones I have set aside and decide which to use as my starter. Sometimes it is three different views of the same place that I work from. Occasionally I will put two slides into the viewer at once to see if the complexity of the confused images is more exciting than either by itself.

I seem to need outside stimulus to get me creating. I envy the artists who carry their images deep within and can produce them entirely from their imagination or their subconscious. But there's not much profit in bemoaning the talents I don't have. It seems wiser to accept my own kind of talent and develop it as far as I can. My work has broken new ground within an honourable tradition, and I have learned at last not to feel guilty because it is not revolutionary. I am grateful that other people have called my vision personal and have seen it as original. Their appreciation is a reassurance that my service to the god is not in vain.

The "Doctor English" hanging at St. Aidan's.

The artist at work, her brushes stuck in the snow.
(Courtesy Wendy Wacko)

Personal encounter with icebergs, Grise Fiord, 1976.

John Scullion at
Pond Inlet, 1972.

Doris and Nan Wright on the edge of the tar sands,
Fort McMurray, 1980.

Nan Wright and Barbara Greene at Back Harbour,
Newfoundland, 1978.

By the igloo that we built at Arctic Bay, 1974.

Reunion at Jasper: Wendy Laughlin Wacko and Barbara Greene, June 1977.

Doris, Bar, and Nan in the badlands, April 1982.

Richard Leiterman filming the subject for *Heart of a Painter*, April 1982.

Wendy Wacko at the reception after the screening of *Heart of a Painter* at Canada House, London, 1983.

The Knothole cottage and studio at Georgian Bay.

Florence Smedley immortalizing the bay.

Showing off on ice.

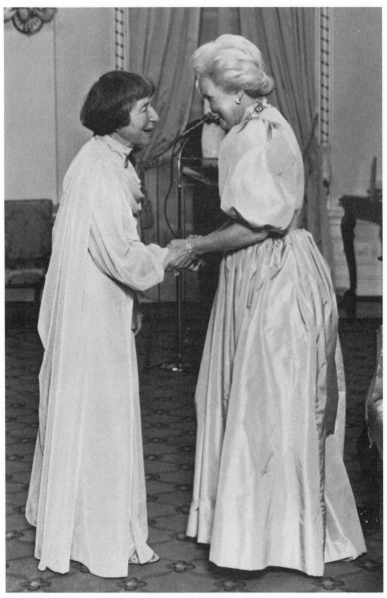

Honoured by the Order of Canada from the hands of Governor
General Madame Sauvé, 1987.

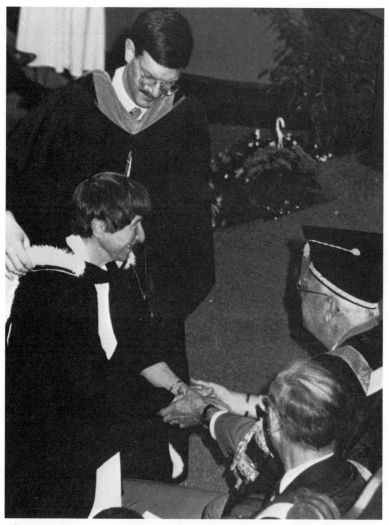

The convocation ceremonies at the University of Toronto, 1989.

Fool's Paradise, better every year. *(Courtesy Brigette Schreyer)*

11

Retrospect

THE WINTER AFTERNOON IN 1986 that the meteorite landed on my head (by registered mail, I having received a postcard telling me to call at Station B to collect it) I was due in at Marjorie Dickinson's to tear down her decrepit picket fence and load it into the car to be cut up for firewood. My brother Douglas lives just a block away from her and came over to help me. Since Audrey's death in 1978 left Doug alone, I have seen far more of him, finding him a willing ally and a good companion, with a sharp mind and a quiet wit that is appreciated by my friends.

I arrived with the letter in my purse and a strong sense of unreality, but I couldn't tell Marjorie or Doug about it. I pulled the fence apart and broke up the pieces in a daze.

"I am pleased to inform you, in confidence, that the Governor General has received a recommendation for your appointment as a Member of the Order of Canada," and at the end, "You will, I am sure, understand that this matter should be held in strict confidence until the official announcement is made."

The secret was safe with me for the long month or so to New Year's, when the list would be published. I would nurse this delicious knowledge like an infant at my breast. Christmas that year was heightened by the thought that the New Year was only a week away, but New Year's Day brought no honours list. I scoured the paper in vain. Two weeks later I received a letter of confirmation and felt free to tell my loved ones. They reacted with predictable pleasure, and once again I began to watch the papers eagerly. When the announcement did appear, the only person to see it was Andrew Patenall, dear Andrew Patenall, my Shakespeare professor and friend, who telephoned with a most gratifying enthusiasm. But if the reaction was slow, it was mounting. The first trickle of phone calls became a flood; letters and cards began to arrive in ones or twos; there were press calls and photographers' appointments. The best fun was at my exhibition opening at Wynick/Tuck that spring. Everyone came. Marjorie Dickinson catered to the gallery's very special reception and provided a huge cake with the insignia of the Order in icing on the top. That was a heady day.

Doug came with me to the investiture at Ottawa, which was a gracious, dignified ceremony, a leisurely and repetitive ritual, interesting, and meticulously organized. Nothing could go wrong, and nothing did. My experience with theatre gives me a real appreciation of anything stage-managed so well. For me it was a particular pleasure that the governor general was Madame Sauvé. She was the patron of the Canadian Society of Painters in Water Colour, and had attended our sixtieth anniversary dinner at the Arts and Letters Club in Toronto in 1986. That was the year the queen accepted sixty water-colours by members of the society to be in the permanent collection of the library of Windsor Castle. I had been put next to Madame Sauvé at dinner, probably as the oldest active past-president, and had found her charming and easy to be with. At the investiture it was like receiving the medal from a friend.

Every new member of the Order is sent a photograph taken by a professional at the very moment of the presentation. If we had been rehearsed and posed with retake after retake we could hardly have achieved anything more felicitous. The setting is the high-ceilinged ballroom of Rideau Hall, with grey walls and tall windows draped in turquoise satin. Madame Sauvé was wearing grey taffeta that reflected the light of the chandeliers and the colour of the drapes. Her hair was silver. My gown (that was no mere dress!) was a turquoise sheath, floor length, with an over-drape of sheer silver lamé. We were in animated conversation, both smiling. After the Arctic Bay igloo, this is my next favourite photograph.

That was the year that I had chosen creative writing as one of the courses to take at Scarborough College. About fifteen of us, men and women, young and not so young, gathered in the classroom with the yellow swivel chairs to take turns reading an original poem for the rest to receive critically or appreciatively or both. We learned a bit about each other and perhaps more about ourselves, as well as something about today's voice. In the second term we were writing fiction. The only script I submitted that met with much enthusiasm was a sketch of a day in the Arctic, biographical rather than fictional. Russell Brown, the professor, recommended that I do more such. I was carrying another English course as well, writing essays and papers, and taking them to Doug for typing. It did make for delays while I copied the work into legible form and gave him time to type it. I decided that I should move into the twentieth century, buy myself a word-processor, and learn to use it.

Nothing in my whole life was as frustrating, humiliating, and difficult as learning to master that servant. The instructions came in a strange, repellent language. When I summoned courage to tap a key to make it do what I thought it was supposed to do, on the screen would appear an obscure message, such as, "Error, Doris, change the default drive and try again." To be reproached by name added to my embarrassment. I struggled on for months. I think it was Lorie's wedding that brought Fran Bennett to Toronto and Fool's Paradise that spring, but come she did, and sat down in front of my machine, played with it for a while, and left me with clear directions, in intelligible English, how to "boot it up," write a document, and, most important of all, preserve what I had written and keep it available.

Some of my self-confidence returned when I discovered that my machine had some factory flaws in it and all the confusion was not my fault. I have learned to love it dearly. They tell me that children in grade two take to computers as naturally as to dolls and toy guns.

Since I can't bear waste, it was inevitable that I should

sign up for a second year of creative writing to use what
I had learned with so much travail. Advanced creative
writing was on a one-to-one basis, which meant that I had
to find a professor willing to work with me. The two
English courses that I had taken with Alan Thomas
taught me that he was hard to please and a tough marker.
I trusted him. I asked him if he would take me, and
suggested that I would like to go on with autobiographical
sketches as recommended by Russell Brown. Every other
Tuesday I would meet Alan in his office, hand him two
chapters diffidently, and sit in tense silence while he read
them. I was lucky if there were only two mistakes in
spelling, and delighted if he gave a snort here and there
over an anecdote. His criticisms were perceptive and
helpful, and I would drive home to a late tea with Fran
Dalziel exhilarated and eager to get on with it.

Writing this autobiography has been a wonderfully
rewarding experience. It drove me back to the diaries that
have been idle on my shelves for years and made me relive
the passions, the heartbreak, and the raptures. It gave me
back my girlhood, the years when I was discovering my
artist's eye and the heady joy of creation. I suffered again
through my thirties, when I was desperate with frustrated
love and when too briefly I knew fulfilment. Writing of
those days, recording my wonderful year with Ginny and
my development as an artist since that time, was being
given a second chance, not to change things, but to savour
them and to appreciate how good the years have been.

A half-course on biography the following term completed my undergraduate work, let me become (proud
moment) a BA Hons., and introduced me to a variety of
other lives and how they were recorded. It also shook my

confidence in the trustworthiness of autobiographies. We were led to see that the writer himself often may not realize his own evasions and rationalizations. You have been warned.

Keeping cats (if anyone can be said to *keep* a cat) means that I cannot lock up Fool's Paradise and just take off. When I go away on a painting trip or up to Georgian Bay, there has to be someone here to feed and water and love them. Since Ginty died I have had many and varied deputies, some for a week or two, some for several consecutive years, all of them learning to feel a proprietary affection for the place. This pleases me. I have never felt as if I owned Fool's Paradise. Like my paintings, it is something that I create to give more life to others and to me. My latest cat-sitter, Lynne Atkinson, came three years ago and by mutual consent at the end of the summer stayed on, becoming family. She is a gardener and has taken over the house-plants entirely. Although many decades apart in age, we are compatible, sharing a love of mornings, of solitude, and of people. Each of us has a busy, independent, and full life, all the pleasanter when our orbits occasionally cross.

The road to Fool's Paradise plunges down a steep wooded hill to a narrow plateau that runs along the top of Scarborough Bluffs. The shore below it is the very beach on which my father and I landed for our picnic together when I was eleven years old. A few yards out in the lake the landmark wreck still breaks the surface of the water and reminds me of Dad. In the early days, before the trees had grown and the vacant land had been

built on, we named it Meadowcliff Drive, an accurate
description. (I continue stubbornly to spell cliff the way
the dictionary does, although even the street signs have
added an *e*.) The plateau is bounded by two ravines, both
now parkland. On the east side of my house is the Bellamy
Ravine, which used to be partly wooded and partly raw
clay and sand bluffs. When I first moved here I estimated
that the trickle of water that ran down the centre had been
creating the ravine all through the ten thousand years
since the last ice age. The ravine had grown wider at the
rate of about six inches a century. Deer visited it sometimes, and came up into the little woods at the lake end
of my land. A red fox raised a family in those woods a
year ago. I suspect she is the reason that all the pheasants
have disappeared. They used to be common. Rabbits,
squirrels, skunks, and coons are dependable regulars,
although the groundhogs far outnumber them. I sit on the
patio in summer and watch their heads popping up and
down in the field, and see the bold little beast that lives
under the house scampering past, or gnawing away at the
chrysanthemum plants in the garden.

The original, very deep ravine began getting dramatically deeper and wider after the war. All the farmland that
used to lie for miles around us was subdivided during the
forties, covered with houses, and the roads and driveways
paved. The rain that used to seep harmlessly into the
ground began to run off the roofs and pavements and rush
through culverts into the head of Bellamy Ravine, cours-
ing down the centre of the gully, gouging out the bottom,
undermining the cliffs on each side, and churning over
the trees that fell from the slopes. Between Fran Dalziel's
house and mine, both on the ravine, a gulch began to

form. Originally, wells and septic tanks balanced each
other. After the war, wells were replaced by city water,
all of which went eventually into the septic tanks and had
to find its way out through the soil. It flowed underground until it could find a hard layer to take it to the face
of the bluffs or the ravine. A steady stream of underground water emptied between Fran's house and mine.
Every winter the face of the ravine froze hard, and the
seepage water was held back and built up pressure. Come
spring, it thawed, and the outrush of water carried away
a whole layer of the face with it. Our flat land had been
falling into the ravine so quickly that we feared for our
houses.

We watched each tree collapse and each foot of land
crumble away. I dismantled the fence section by section
as the edge crept closer. We hired a consultant engineer,
who did soil tests and took photographs but offered little
hope that anything we could do would be effective. One
of my friends suggested that I should pray about it, and
made me realize how little right I had to ask God to work
a miracle to stop the erosion in Bellamy Ravine.

Perhaps even thinking about this, as Fran and I did
together, gave us the will to do something ourselves. We
financed her youngest son, Gordon, who was a student
at Ryerson Polytechnical College, to get a team of lads to
help him line the stream-bed where it passed below our
lands, using gabions to contain the water. The Metro
Conservation Authority gave us permission to do the
work and kept a concerned eye on its progress.

A gabion, as I learned, is a coffin-sized wire basket,
which comes flat but is pulled out into shape and then
filled with stones too big to spill out of the mesh. Gabions

are used like huge blocks, put side by side or piled one on top of another and then wired together for extra stability. After trying many unsuccessful ways to deliver the stones into the ravine, the boys finally rigged up a two-bucket pulley, with an empty bucket zooming up as a full one swung down. The ravine was so deep and steep that the boys themselves needed a rope to help them up and down.

But what a beautiful sight it was to see the stone-lined watercourse, and the stream contained within it. We enjoyed it until the spring floods rolled the gabions out of position as if they had been made of wicker and left them this-way-that-way half-covered with fresh mud. The second year saw the team back on the job, doubling the number of gabions in the walls and adding buttress gabions at right angles every few feet for further strength.

Even before the gabion work, Fran had held an annual tree-planting when her young people, their friends, and their in-laws had spent a Saturday in May setting out a thousand seedlings in the hope of getting growth re-established along the slopes. The grey-haired worked with the grandchildren on the steep clay bank, with the rope to help climb up over the verge. Every year a few of the trees survived and even flourished. If the planting didn't do anything permanent for the ravine, it built clan solidarity and was a good party.

All this was just to buy time in hopes that some action would be taken by government at some level to undo the damage that had been done by putting this extra water into the ravine. To avoid expropriation, we were willing to do anything we could to help them to help us. And at last Scarborough did recognize the scale of the effort we had made at our own expense.

As I write this, the dump trucks are going BANG BANG BANG in the ravine. Two bulldozers have been at work five days a week for three years. A great blue and yellow monster with a long flexible neck and a bucket of a mouth is gnawing here and spitting back there to shape the earth that is being dumped by the hundred truckloads daily. The level of the bottom is being raised. On top of the fill a watercourse is being built, lined with huge stones, each block as big as a gabion. Below the stones is a layer of filter blanket, and the sides of the ravine are being graded to the angle of repose. Deeding ten of my thirteen acres to the Metro Conservation Authority was a small price to pay for the sense of security they have given me. They will not only halt the erosion but create a wooded valley with an open stream-bed in a setting of grass and trees. A footpath will give public access to the beach. In another year the seeding and planting should be finished, and birdsong and quiet will once more be our neighbours.

To me this means that Fool's Paradise will continue to be a refuge for whoever needs sanctuary, a place for healing, for laughter, for shared tears, for growing.

I spend a good deal of my life tidying, putting things away, restoring order. Last year I tackled the job of tidying my affairs – affairs in the financial sense, the only kind I have these days. I revised my will after finding out from my family and young friends which of my possessions they would like to have, so as to give my executors as easy a time as possible. I am planning to make my funeral a celebration rather than a time of grief. It seems important to me to give some thought to death so that it can be received graciously, like any other guest.

I thank Mother for the strong constitution that lets me be so vigorous at eighty. I choose to keep my hair from showing white, and work at standing up straight and moving quickly, which fools some people into thinking I am younger than I am, unless the light is good and the wrinkles show. My doctor gives the credit to my routine of skating, my healthy diet, and my zest for life. My worst symptom of aging, worse than wrinkles, is my loss of hearing. I remember one gallery opening where I heard one of the women near me say, "She's not quite a virgin, though she has some virgin in her." This intrigued me, and I moved close enough to realize that the lady under discussion was an almost-Persian cat. Ginny and I have each become deaf in one ear, a disability that makes cocktail parties or any large gathering a bit of a hazard but provides us with many a laugh when we are together and discover what the other actually heard or said.

Our favourite story is of the two old boys on the English train. "Was that Wembley?" "No, it's Thursday." "So am I. Let's have a drink." The great thing about having friends of your own age is laughing together about the shared disabilities.

I remember with some amusement that when I retired from teaching almost twenty years ago, I thought with a sense of shock and even dismay that the next major event in my life would be dying. There was no imagining then that the best years of my life were still ahead of me. In fact every decade has been better than the one just gone, and already the nineties have brought unexpected gifts and prospects of more good things to come.

Early in 1991 I went off to the Antarctic to see if it could compete with the Canadian north in beauty and interest. I found it different and yet the same, with penguins as a new and piquant note. Shortly after my return I settled into St. Michael's Printshop in St. John's, Newfoundland, for an absorbing month learning to make lithographs, with a master printer at my elbow to provide the expertise and the muscle to handle the stones. This last summer has seen the fulfilment of every artist's dream, a major retrospective exhibition at a public gallery and with a worthy catalogue. And for me the icing on the cake was its location in Stratford, Stratford of such rich memories. The exhibition opened at the Gallery/Stratford in May for the first of its scheduled showings at galleries across Canada. And this part two of my autobiography will be launched at my 1991 exhibition of current work at the Wynick/Tuck Gallery in Toronto.

So here I am, enjoying every day as it comes, healthy (very healthy for my age), wealthy (very wealthy by my Depression-conditioned standards), and wise enough to thank God for his mercies and rejoice in them.

Index

Page references in italic are to the first volume of these memoirs, *A Fool in Paradise*; references in roman are to *The Good Wine*.

This book was typeset by Tony Gordon Limited in Cochin, a typeface that originated with the Peignot Foundry in Paris about 1915. It is based on the lettering of eighteenth-century French copperplate engravers. In America, Monotype adapted it in 1917, followed by ATF in 1925. Today it is available both in phototypesetting and as an Adobe face. The roman is distinctive but the italic even more so, being closer to formal handwriting or engraving than most italics.

Book design by Linda Gustafson

Printed on acid-free paper by John Deyell Company